The God
Squad

The God Squad
The Born-Again San Francisco Giants of 1978
Copyright © 2023 by Matt Sieger

All rights reserved. No part of this book may be reproduced or transmitted in any form or by any means without written permission from the publisher and author.

Additional copies may be ordered from the publisher for educational, business, promotional or premium use.
For information, contact ALIVE Book Publishing at:
alivebookpublishing.com

Book and cover design by Alex P. Johnson

ISBN 13
978-1-63132-207-5 Deluxe Color Paperback
978-1-63132-218-1 Standard Paperback

Library of Congress Control Number: 2023916738

Library of Congress Cataloging-in-Publication Data
is available upon request.

First Edition

Published in the United States of America by ALIVE Book Publishing and ALIVE Publishing Group, imprints of Advanced Publishing LLC
3200 A Danville Blvd., Suite 204, Alamo, California 94507
alivebookpublishing.com

PRINTED IN THE UNITED STATES OF AMERICA

10 9 8 7 6 5 4 3 2 1

The God Squad

The Born-Again
San Francisco Giants of 1978

Matt Sieger

ABOOKS
Alive Book Publishing

This book is dedicated to my mother, Jeanette, who lived to be one hundred and never stopped believing in me.

CONTENTS

Chapter 1	A Tale of One City	9
Chapter 2	The Born-Again Year	15
Chapter 3	The Lieutenant	35
Chapter 4	Bob Knepper	43
Chapter 5	Rob Andrews	53
Chapter 6	Jack Clark	59
Chapter 7	BOO!	71
Chapter 8	Mike Ivie	79
Chapter 9	The Other Guys	93
Chapter 10	God's Will	103
Chapter 11	The Killer Instinct	129
Chapter 12	Jesus at the Bat	155
Chapter 13	Satan and the Giants	167
Chapter 14	Understanding Lowell Cohn	177
Chapter 15	Scapegoats	187
Chapter 16	Baseball Chapel	203
Chapter 17	God Squad Sunset	215
Chapter 18	God Squad II	223
Chapter 19	Satan and Brett Butler	235
Chapter 20	God Squad III?	245
Afterword		249
Acknowledgments		251
About the Author		255

Chapter 1
A Tale of One City

With sincere apologies to Charles Dickens: It was the best of times, it was the worst of times, it was the Age of Aquarius, it was the age of Watergate, it was the epoch of sexual freedom, it was the epoch of self-denial, it was the season of Transcendental Meditation, it was the season of hallucinogenic medication, it was the advent of legal abortion, it was the advent of the Moral Majority, it was a time of war, it was a time of protests, it was the decade of forced busing, it was the decade of White Flight, it was a period of individualism, it was a period of doing what everybody else did.

This was the 1970s in America. In San Francisco, the contrasts were even more stark. The city accepted diverse cultures and welcomed hippies, radicals, and the LGBT community. At the same time, drugs, prostitution, and crime were rampant.

The San Francisco sound, unleashed in the mid-1960s by rock groups such as the Grateful Dead, Jefferson Airplane, and Big Brother and the Holding Company (with Janis Joplin), expanded into the 1970s. But the city was the center of the pornography industry, with the proliferation of adult movie theaters, strip clubs, and sex shops.

A group of Native Americans ushered in the decade with a nineteen-month long occupation of Alcatraz Island, bringing international attention to the plight of native peoples in the United States.

But the worst soon overtook the best. In the late 1960s and early 1970s, the Zodiac Killer terrified local residents. In 1973 and 1974, the Zebra Killings, a series of murders of white people by radical African-Americans, terrorized the city. In 1974, the Symbionese Liberation Army kidnapped Patty Hearst, who then participated with her captors in the armed robbery of a San Francisco bank. In November 1978, Harvey Milk, the first openly gay male politician elected to the San Francisco Board of Supervisors, was assassinated, along with Mayor George Moscone, by former police officer and Board of Supervisor member Dan White. That same month, Jim Jones, the leader of the Peoples Temple in San Francisco, led more than nine hundred of his members in a mass murder-suicide in their compound, Jonestown, in Guyana.

The 1970s were a time of spiritual searching. Eastern religions made inroads in the U.S., with Hare Krishnas and Moonies seeking adherents. Zen Buddhism attracted the interest of young Americans. So did Scientology, EST, and Synanon. In 1966 Timothy Leary told young people to "turn on, tune in, drop out," and LSD became a supposed shortcut to spiritual enlightenment. In the mix was the Jesus Revolution, whose impact was evidenced by plays and movies like *Godspell* and *Jesus Christ Superstar*.

The Jesus movement started in Southern California in the late 1960s. It intertwined with the hippie movement, as young people were seeking an individual spirituality that challenged traditional practice. Jesus, a revolutionary in his day, was an attractive personality. While Jesus was "just all right" with the Doobie Brothers, for many young people he became the one they followed wholeheartedly.

Those who did were labeled "born-again," a reference to a passage in the New Testament where Jesus tells a Jewish seeker, "Truly, truly, I say to you, unless someone is born again he cannot see the kingdom of God."[1]

It wasn't just hippies who were swept up in the Jesus wave. Many young people, some raised in traditional churches, were looking for something more authentic, a personal relationship with a God who cared for them.

So it should have been no big surprise when several members of the San Francisco Giants became born-again Christians in the mid-to-late 1970s. But their openness about their newfound faith, along with its attendant moral values, created the perfect storm in a San Francisco which championed abortion rights, gay rights, sexual freedom, and the legalization of drugs.

In 1978 the team had an unexpectedly outstanding year, challenging the Los Angeles Dodgers and Cincinnati Reds for the division title until the final month of the season in an exciting pennant race. Some of the players were vocal about their faith during interviews, crediting God for the ability he gave them, which led to questioning by the Bay Area media. Two newspaper columnists in particular, Lowell Cohn and Glenn Dickey, both of the *San Francisco Chronicle*, wrote some provocative pieces about the God Squadders.

It is difficult to track down when the term "God Squad" was first used to denote the born-again players on the Giants. In a 1981 *New York Times* article, George Vecsey claimed the term was coined in 1978.[2] But the first instance of the precise term "God Squad" that this author found was in an Art Rosenbaum column in the Sunday *San Francisco Examiner and Chronicle* on July 1, 1979, titled "Faith, Hope and Sports." He wrote, "The Giants are the 'God Squad' of baseball. Eight have been born again and the number could increase to ten."[3]

The headline for an article by Bob Slocum about the Giants in *The Modesto* (California) *Bee* in August 1978 was "God's Squad." But "God's Squad" is not the same as "God Squad," and Slocum used neither term in the body of the article.[4]

That the term was used primarily as a pejorative when the Giants struggled on the diamond in 1979 is supported by Terence Moore, who wrote for the *Examiner* at the time. In a 1989 article for the *Atlanta Journal-Constitution*, he wrote, "In 1978, the San Francisco Giants nearly captured the NL West with Bob Knepper, Gary Lavelle, Jack Clark, and Rob Andrews among their key players. They were frequently referred to as 'outspoken Christian players' that season but when the Giants flopped the following year, fans, teammates and members of the local media derisively called them 'The God Squad.'"[5]

When the Giants staggered in 1979 and 1980 to fourth and fifth place finishes, respectively, some sportswriters averred that the God Squadders lost their competitive edge after becoming Christians, a charge which the born-again players vigorously refuted. A notorious claim by the media was that after giving up a game-winning home run, Bob Knepper said it was "God's will." Knepper strongly denies ever having said that, and this author has been unable to find the quote in newspaper archives.

Cohn employed satire in speaking about the Christian Giants. Although those columns were humorous to many, his targets did not always appreciate them. Dickey was more heavy-handed and at one point even called on the Giants to trade one or two of the more prominent Christians "to break up that clique."[6]

Rosenbaum of the *Chronicle* generally allowed the born-again Giants to give their point of view without injecting his own. Prominent *Chronicle* columnist Herb Caen took occasional pot shots at the God Squad.

Cohn, Dickey, and the God Squadders were often at odds, which made for some interesting reading but also caused the born-again Giants to mistrust the press. Cohn felt the tension, and in his memoirs made this fascinating statement: "Until that day, I believed I was covering a baseball team. I was wrong. I had wandered into the middle of a deep religious debate, one that defined the Giants at that time."[7]

Mike Granberry of the *Los Angeles Times* wrote:

[Mike] Ivie has speculated that maybe he and his teammates received more of their share of attention as "born-agains" because of the image of San Francisco. How incongruous for a team to have not one but several outspoken crusaders in a city so cosmopolitan and urbane.

"It's a different city," Ivie has said, and perhaps he was right. You hear about the so-called "God Squadders" in Dallas, but San Francisco?[8]

Who were these God Squadders? The members of the 1978 team whose faith was most discussed in the two major San Francisco newspapers, the morning *Chronicle* and the afternoon *Examiner*, were Lavelle, Knepper, Andrews, Clark, Ivie, and Johnnie LeMaster. Other born-again Giants who were less vocal with the media about their faith included Terry Whitfield, Bill Madlock, Marc Hill, Larry Herndon, and Randy Moffitt. Widely different in background and personality, their common faith united them. They needed that bond in what became a test of their faith in a city that loved its Giants but was divided on how to respond to these players who wanted to talk about Jesus.

Notes

[1] John 3:3. New American Standard Bible.

[2] George Vecsey, "Religion Becomes an Important Part of Baseball Scene," *The New York Times*, May 10, 1981, Section 5, 1.

[3] Art Rosenbaum, "Faith, Hope and Sports," *San Francisco Examiner*, July 1, 1979, 114.

[4] Bob Slocum, "God's Squad," *The Modesto Bee*, August 13, 1978, 51.

[5] Terence Moore, "Baseball and Religion," *Atlanta Journal-Constitution*, August 13,1989, C-1.

[6] Glenn Dickey, "Time to Think About Next Year," *San Francisco Chronicle*, August 13, 1979, 48.

[7] Lowell Cohn, *Gloves Off: 40 Years of Unfiltered Sportswriting* (Petaluma, CA: Roundtree Press, 2020), 126.

[8] Mike Granberry, "The Season According to Jack Clark," *Los Angeles Times*, April 10, 1980, 32, 35.

Chapter 2
The Born-Again Year

As the 1978 season approached, there was little reason to believe the Giants would be competitive in the National League West. After the team relocated from New York to San Francisco in 1958, the Giants had only made the post-season twice. In 1962 they lost to the New York Yankees in the World Series in seven games. In 1971 they won their division but fell to the Pittsburgh Pirates in the National League Championship Series, three games to one. The Pirates went on to win the World Series.

The last time the Giants had posted a better than .500 record was 1973. Owner Horace Stoneham sold the team to Bob Lurie in 1976. By that time, the stars that had brought the fans to Candlestick Park—Willie Mays, Willie McCovey, Orlando Cepeda, Gaylord Perry, and Juan Marichal—had been traded. Candlestick Park, with its swirling winds and freezing temperatures, was at least partly responsible for the dwindling attendance. The Giants were twenty-fifth in attendance in 1977 out of the twenty-six major league teams.

New ownership did not seem to be making a difference. The Giants finished fourth in the West in 1976 and 1977, with records of 74–88 and 75–87, respectively. McCovey was re-signed in 1977, which lifted everyone's spirits a bit, but it wasn't enough to inspire much hope for 1978.

But just before the 1978 interleague trading deadline, which fell in March at that time, the Giants traded with the Oakland A's for Vida Blue, the Cy Young and MVP award winner and three-time All-Star who helped the A's win three consecutive world championships.

"When they went out and got Vida Blue, we all got really excited then," McCovey said. "That was all we needed . . . The pitchers were all young, and Vida gave them that veteran leadership."[1]

The starting rotation had two tough lefties, Blue and Knepper, and two hard-throwing righthanders, John Montefusco and Ed Halicki. Short relievers (the term "closer" wasn't in use yet), right-hander Moffitt and southpaw Lavelle, and swing man Jim Barr made for a solid bullpen.

When Halicki went on the disabled list during spring training, Barr became the fourth starter, then was used in relief when Halicki returned on May 14. As a starting pitcher from 1973 to 1977 with the Giants, Barr finished in the National League's top ten three times for earned run average and shutouts and twice for complete games and innings pitched,

In 1978, Blue led the staff with eighteen victories, followed by Knepper with seventeen, including six shutouts. Knepper, Blue, and Halicki finished fourth, fifth, and sixth, respectively, in the National League in earned run average.

"Because of our pitching," Knepper said, "there was never a game that season we didn't think we could win."[2]

Montefusco added, "The thing that made us so good, is that we were so competitive with each other."[3]

In his first start of the season at Cincinnati, Knepper pitched six innings, yielding two runs, and Lavelle came on for three scoreless innings to notch the win, which was secured by an eighth-inning solo home run by Clark to beat the Reds, 3–2. The born-again Giants were beginning to make their mark on the field.

The 1978 Giants were also much more aggressive on the basepaths, having brought in famed base-stealer Maury Wills as a special coach in spring training.

"Early in the season we went to San Diego and just ran rings around the Padres, taking every extra base," said Knepper. "We were a bunch of young guys having a good time, and I remember thinking this is what baseball is all about."[4]

The Giants only played .500 baseball in April, but one highlight was a Knepper complete-game, three-hit shutout of the Cincinnati Reds to beat Hall of Fame pitcher Tom Seaver at Candlestick on April 21. Knepper struck out ten batters, including three consecutive punch-outs of feared Cincinnati slugger George Foster.

"I've never done anything better in my life," said Knepper, "It's the greatest thing to happen to me since I got married."[5]

The *Chronicle* game story noted, "LeMaster was a master at shortstop making one particularly breathtaking throw from the deep hole to throw out Seaver."[6]

The Giants started to gel and took the division lead over the Reds by .005 percentage points on May 12 when Blue won his fifth straight game, beating the Cardinals 9-3, while Madlock and Whitfield hit back-to-back home runs. San Francisco beat the Cards the next day, 7–6, with a double by Ivie driving in two runs and a triple by Clark scoring Ivie in the decisive seventh inning, Lavelle getting the save. San Francisco then won both games in extra innings against St. Louis in a Sunday Candlestick doubleheader. That completed a four-game sweep of the Cards and increased their division lead to 1 ½ games over the Reds and two games over the Dodgers. Lavelle got the win in the first game, and

Clark, Hill, and Whitfield homered, the latter a walk-off blast with two outs in the twelfth inning. In the second game, Hill pinch-hit a single in the tenth inning with two outs to drive in the winning run.

Relief pitcher Greg Minton, who was optioned to the Giants' Phoenix AAA minor league team when Halicki came off the disabled list, noticed something during his short stay with the parent club.

"You know," said Minton, "I feel really comfortable with the Giants this year. There's no bickering or squabbling like last year. Everybody is slightly keyed up because we know we can beat the other teams."[7]

On May 23 Leonard Koppett wrote in *The New York Times*, "Manager Joe Altobelli's current group has more team unity, more star quality (in Blue, Madlock, and McCovey) and more promising youth (in Clark, Knepper, and Terry Whitfield) than its predecessors."[8]

By late May, the fans started coming back to Candlestick. After the Giants beat the Dodgers on May 26, 6–1, McCovey, who drove in five runs, three on a home run, said, "I can't say enough about the fans. They're getting behind us and it feels great."[9] Clark, who extended his consecutive game hitting streak to sixteen with a double and a single, added, "We're starting to play like we're unbeatable at home."[10]

The *Eureka Times Standard* reported, "Sister Margaret, who teaches first grade at St. Joseph's school in San Francisco, told Giants announcer Lon Simmons that she has her students say prayers, recite the Pledge of Allegiance to the flag and sing the Giants fight song before class."[11]

Candlestick had a record crowd of 56,103 on May 28 when the Giants erased a 5-0 Los Angeles Dodgers lead and won 6–5, fueled by a pinch-hit grand slam home run from

Mike Ivie. The Giants had been trailing 3–0 going into the bottom of the sixth inning. After the team scored once and loaded the bases, Ivie drilled a shot over the left-field wall to put them ahead 5–3.

The *Chronicle* reported:

> *The deafening Candlestick reception for Ivie's home run was what Montefusco wanted to discuss. "I was talking to (trainer) Joe Liscio when Mike got up there and said, 'Wouldn't it be unbelievable if he hit one out?' Joe then says, 'He's gonna do it on this pitch.' And sure enough, he did. The ovation Mike got was something I'll never forget. We're going right down to the wire with the Dodgers in every game we play."*
>
> *Ivie, sent up to bat for left-handed Vic Harris in an against-the-percentage move [because the pitcher, Don Sutton, is right-handed], said he was "just looking for a fly ball" against Sutton with one out. "He gave me something I could pull, but I didn't think it was going out. Then the crowd told me it was. The whole feeling is beyond words."*[12]

Giants fan Charles A. Fracchia Jr., who was thirteen and at the game that day, said, "He [Ivie] nails that pitch over the fence . . . The whole stadium rocks like it was an earthquake. The stadium shook. It was unreal. People hugging each other . . . such excitement."[13]

The *Examiner* reported:

> *"I tell ya, this team has so much confidence in each other," said Ivie . . . "If we get behind we know we can come back. We believe so much that we can do it. It's a feeling that no other club in the major leagues has got. We have a home-*

type unity-type of feeling. It's super. I don't want to be anyplace else but here. Now I don't want you to misunderstand this but if we go on the road and win some games I really believe in my heart that we can win the whole thing."[14]

Whitfield added, "We feel in ourselves we can do it. Comebacks like this prove it. If it happened another time, well, then, we can do it again."[15]

After that game, Larry Keith of *Sports Illustrated* wrote, "Fourth a year ago, the Giants have not had a winning record in five seasons, a million-plus gate in seven or a pennant in 16. Nob Hill had become Sob Hill. But league-leading pitching and timely hitting are starting to change all that, and Candlestick Park, once a cold, lonely outpost, is suddenly red hot with excitement."[16]

Keith closed his article with quotes from a couple of Giants: " 'The Dodgers and Reds have the prestige of the past, but this is today,' says Whitfield. 'We're young, they're getting old.' Adds Montefusco, 'I used to have to lie a little to get the fans to come out. Now I really believe we are good. I finally feel like I'm in the big leagues.' "[17]

The next night in Houston, after the Giants defeated the Astros, Houston manager Bill Virdon said, "I don't think the Giants have the talent of the other clubs [the Dodgers and Reds]. But that's a compliment to them for where they are right now. I don't think they can last the whole season. But if they do, I'll take my hat off to them."[18]

The following night, Knepper pitched a complete game, five-hit, 1–0 win over the Astros and drove in the game's only run with a sacrifice fly. He defeated Houston's formidable pitcher, James Rodney Richard, who limited the Giants to three hits. The win increased Knepper's record to

7–2, lowered his ERA to 2.01, and gave the Giants a 2 ½ game lead over the Cincinnati Reds.

After the game, Madlock said, "I think right now he's the best lefty in the league. And I think we've got the one-two lefthanders with Knepper and [Vida] Blue. When you talk about lefthanders you look at [Steve] Carlton and [Jerry] Koosman and [John] Candelaria. None of them is pitching anywhere near as well as Knepper and Blue."[19]

The next day, Herb Caen wrote in his *Chronicle* column, "The team is indeed For Real. It's a miracle to see crowds at Candlestick. I walk a little straighter, knowing we is 'Numbah One!' "[20]

On June 16 at Candlestick, the Giants staged an improbable ninth-inning rally, tying the game on a pinch-hit homer from Hector Cruz, who had just arrived in San Francisco that day after being traded by the Cubs. Then Lavelle, remaining in the game now that the score was tied, was allowed to hit and delivered a single, only the third hit in his major league career. After an intentional walk to Darrell Evans, Jack Clark smacked a home run to give the Giants a 7–4 victory over the Mets.

Stephanie Salter wrote in the *Examiner*, "In real life, when a team is down 4-3 in the bottom of the ninth and its newest player gets up to hit, he strikes out. The Giants are not in the real world. This season they are in a strange dimension where corny and ridiculous happy endings are the rule rather than the exception and the scripts are played out to the tune of 'The Impossible Dream.' "[21]

W.A. Van Winkle echoed Salter's thoughts in the *San Francisco Bay Guardian*:

> ... *someone will appear from the bench or out of the bullpen*

and drive in the winning run—despite a low batting average, a hitting slump or near-blindedness. Someone will walk in from the bullpen and retire each of the last nine batters to preserve a win. Someone will steal a base and put a run in scoring position—last year he would have been thrown out. And someone will hurtle the baseball from the left-field corner all 335 feet to home plate to force the final out of the game.[22]

Giants' manager Joe Altobelli was pressing all the right buttons. The Giants were locked in a tight game with the Padres in San Diego on June 27, San Francisco leading 3–1 heading into the seventh inning. When the Giants loaded the bases, Altobelli pinch hit Clark for Whitfield. Usually that move would not be surprising, since relief pitcher Dennis Kinney is left-handed and Whitfield bats left, while Clark bats right. However, Whitfield was four-for-four on the day. But Altobelli rolled the dice and Clark belted a grand slam to secure the victory for the Giants.

On June 30, Bill Lyon of the *Philadelphia Inquirer* quoted manager Sparky Anderson of the Cincinnati Reds: "I can't think of a team with five better starting pitchers. And they've got Gary Lavelle and Randy Moffitt coming out of the bullpen. That's some staff . . . There's a lot of talk about the Dodgers and us, but there's no way I'm taking the Giants lightly, not with that pitching."[23]

That same day, McCovey made history when he became just the twelfth player to hit five hundred home runs, and Ivie hit his second pinch-hit grand-slam homer of the season.

Clark and Blue were selected to the National League All-Star team, and Blue became the first pitcher to start an All-Star game in both leagues.

At the All-Star break, the Giants were in first place, two games ahead of the Dodgers and three games up on the Reds. After Clark's All-Star selection, national periodicals took notice. *The New York Times*, *Us* magazine, and *The Sporting News* all ran features on the Giants' twenty-two-year-old right fielder.

During the All-Star break, Clark told Dave Anderson of *The New York Times*, "Everybody used to say the Giants have the pitching but not the hitting. But we're hitting about .260 as a team now [third in the league behind the Dodgers and the Reds] . . . We've got good hitters—Bill Madlock, Willie McCovey, Mike Ivie, Darrell Evans, myself, we can hit."[24]

On July 25 at Candlestick, Blue took a shutout and a 1–0 lead into the ninth inning against the Cardinals, but the Redbirds struck for two runs to take the lead. Bob Stevens of the *Chronicle* described the action in the bottom of the frame:

> *The Little Miracle of Candlestick Park, and the Miracle Man, struck again last night. With one out in the ninth and a deeply disappointed crowd of 39,289 shuffling quietly toward the exits, Larry Herndon singled, pinchitter Mike Ivie did his thing—a home run—and the Giants climbed over the St. Louis Cardinals, 3-2. The Giants are 7020 fans short of hitting the million mark in attendance.*[25]

Blue, who struck out ten batters, said, "I love it man, I love it. That Ivie is the greatest. Just the greatest. You know, what happened tonight is the stamp of what will bring a division championship to San Francisco. I know these things happened a lot during my seven years with the A's: a different hero every night: a team at work."[26]

The win increased the Giants lead over the Cincinnati

Reds to 2 ½ games. Clark doubled to extend his hitting streak to twenty-six (it would end the next day). It was Ivie's third pinch-hit home run of the season. It gave him a .391 average for the season as a pinch hitter and a .324 mark overall.

On July 27, with the Giants in first place, two games ahead of the Dodgers and 2 ½ games up on the Reds, Clark said, "No one gave us much of a chance coming out of spring training and I know some players on other teams kidded me when I said at the start of the season that we had as good a chance as the Dodgers and Reds to win the division. No one kids me anymore because we have made believers out of all of them." [27]

After a three-game losing streak in late July dropped the Giants into a tie with Los Angeles for the league lead, San Francisco took a 1 ½ game lead over both the Dodgers and Reds by sweeping a Sunday doubleheader at home against the Chicago Cubs on July 30. Lavelle held the Cubs down in relief in the first game. In the second contest, a 1–0 complete game shutout by Blue, Ivie made a high leaping grab at first to start a double play in the seventh inning and catcher Marc Hill gunned down Ivan DeJesus trying to steal third base in the eighth inning.

After the game, Blue said, "I was amazed Ivie made that play. For Hill—well, he's as good a defensive catcher as I've ever thrown to."[28]

The Giants held onto the division lead through the early days of August. They split a four-game series at home against the Dodgers, Cincinnati taking over first place by .002 percentage points. The four games pulled in 193,954 fans, lifting the Giants' home attendance for the season to 1,289,199, higher than any complete season since 1966. Ron

Fimrite of *Sports Illustrated* covered the series. He wrote of the Giants:

> *With each critical game in a rapidly expiring season they seem to grow more confident. They have established that their pitching, with a staff ERA of 3.14, is the best in their league and probably the best in baseball. And Clark, Madlock, Whitfield and the off-the-bench flash, Mike Ivie, are all hitting better than .300. Obviously they also subscribe to the message crudely inscribed on a wall of the passageway between the Giant clubhouse and dugout: "Nevah Give Up!"*[29]

Fimrite added:

> *And as a team with more than the ordinary complement of born-again Christians—playing in a notoriously sinful city, at that—they appear convinced that the so-called Big Dodger in the Sky who watched so benignly over their opponents a year ago has come over to their side now. Only divine intervention, in the opinion of the devout Ivie, can account for the Giants' penchant for turning adversity to advantage. "Too many things are happening our way," he says, "too many good things. You just have to believe we're being watched."*[30]

In an article tracing the history of the Dodgers-Giants rivalry, Fimrite wrote, "Clearly, Giant baseball is all the rage in the Bay Area again. In saloons and restaurants, on the floors of the brokerage houses, in the North Beach coffeehouses, in the parks and on the Bay, the most pressing question these days is 'What's the score?'"[31]

The Giants went south to Los Angeles on August 10, in first place a half game ahead of Cincinnati and one game up on the Dodgers. *Time* magazine covered the four-game series and wrote:

> . . . *The Giants for most of 1978 have been leading the league in a ding-dong race. Giant fans, regarded as an endangered species likely to be spotted only on beaches, at discos and in therapy groups, are flocking to Candlestick Park, breaking all attendance records (1.3 million, nearly doubled since last year). Now they dance in the stadium after victory, howl for Dodger blood and scream their affection for a new-found love. Pitcher Vida Blue. "Bloo! Bloo! Bloo!"*[32]

After losing the first two games of the series, the Giants were one game back of Los Angeles on August 12 when Knepper matched up against Dodger ace lefty Tommy John. Knepper pitched a complete-game, 3–2 win to draw the Giants dead even with the Dodgers. Ivie and Madlock both homered, Madlock's round-tripper in the seventh inning breaking the 2–2 tie.

The next day Clark singled in a run in the eleventh inning to beat the Dodgers, 7–6, and put the Giants back in first by one game over Los Angeles and 1 1/2 games over the Reds.. Lavelle pitched 3 2/3 innings of scoreless relief.

Time magazine wrote:

> *The fourth game went into extra innings. The Giants stayed alive on a hit by aging Superstar Willie McCovey, indestructible and still explosive at 40, and carried to victory and a renewed fingernail grip on first place by a brand new hero, 22-year-old Born-Again Christian Rightfielder Jack*

> Clark. Said Clark, after singling home the winning run in the eleventh inning: "This was to prove to the Dodgers and the rest of the league that we're for real."[33]

The *Examiner* reported on the Giants' post-game scene:

> The players were smeared with shaving cream and yellow mustard or anything else that could be sprayed. Dodger Stadium's visiting clubhouse, where the wild and crazy Giants were carrying on like so many Steve Martins, was the scene of a spontaneous celebration.
>
> "We haven't won anything yet, but with everybody hollering and cheering, it looks like a World Series in here," Marc Hill said while wiping a mustard-stained check. "I've never seen anything like it in my life."[34]

Clark added, "If there were 20 people who still doubted we are for real, I think we convinced 15 of them."[35]

But the Giants' joy was short-lived. They lost their next two games in Montreal, and the Dodgers took the division lead for good on August 16. After the second loss to the Expos, Jim Kaplan of *Sports Illustrated* wrote:

> After Montreal's Woodie Fryman one-hit the Giants and Vida Blue, San Francisco Manager Joe Altobelli told his young players that it was possible they might never have another chance like this one, so why not seize the opportunity. The Giants then won two straight, one of them on Mike Ivie's fourth pinch homer of the season. "Poison's a worrier," Willie McCovey said of Ivie. "Coming off the bench, he doesn't have time."[36]

Ivie's pinch-hit home run was a two-out, two-run, ninth-inning, game-winning round-tripper off ace closer Tug McGraw to beat the Phils, 6–5. The victory kept the Giants one game back of the Dodgers. Lavelle got the win in relief.

San Francisco, which had fallen behind by as many as 2 ½ games, came within one game of Los Angeles after sweeping a Sunday doubleheader against the Phillies at Candlestick on September 3. Knepper pitched a complete game in the first contest and struck out nine batters in a 4–1 victory.

But that's as close as the Giants would get. The Dodgers pulled away to win the division. The Cincinnati Reds also overtook the Giants, who finished six games out of first.

"A lot of players on that team hadn't been used to the type of success I had with the A's and all the things that surround a pennant race," Blue told the *Examiner*. "I think they got a little tight. It was like we got our foot in the door and all we had to do was take one more step and close the door behind us. Instead, we closed the door on our hand."[37]

He told Glenn Dickey, "I was almost the only player on the team who had been involved in a pennant race . . . Maybe if I'd been an everyday player, I could have done something to help everybody get the feeling of what they had to do, but as a pitcher, I just wasn't involved every day."[38]

"I know people say we choked in the stretch but I don't agree," said Halicki. "We didn't play that great but the Dodgers were just superior in September."[39]

Andrews said, "They [the Dodgers and Reds] were two of the best. We were a group of overachievers, but in the end we just couldn't match up."[40]

McCovey said, "What I remember about 1978 was that we were having fun all of a sudden again. The Giants went through some years when they weren't having any fun.... We really re-created the excitement that had been missing around here."[41]

Knepper echoed that thought: "It was a great, great fun year for everybody. If only we hadn't faltered in the last few weeks, and lost our momentum . . . "[42]

Altobelli said, "We played so well for so long, and had so much glamour exposure, we knew it was going to hurt if we didn't win. We all hurt when we went from one game to nine games out."[43]

Glenn Schwarz of the *Examiner* wrote, "Now that some of the pain has disappeared, however, the Giants and their born-again fans realize that it was a very good year even without a pennant flag to wave. For the first time in a number of Septembers, their optimism about the club's future is not the result of too many refreshments at the corner saloon."[44]

The baseball was exciting, as the Giants won forty-two games by one run (still a major league record) and had eleven walk-off wins. The 1978 home attendance of 1,740,480 nearly equaled the total of the three previous seasons combined and was a million more than 1977.

You might say the Giants franchise had been born-again, although they fell on hard times and did not reach the postseason until 1987. The Christian players who were most vocal about their faith were a big part of the success of that 1978 team. Knepper went 17–11 with a 2.63 ERA. Lavelle won thirteen games in relief and saved fourteen. Clark erupted for twenty-five home runs and ninety-eight RBIs. Ivie hit .308 and batted .387 as a pinch-hitter. LeMaster was solid in the field as the starting shortstop. Andrews played a key role as a utility infielder.

That made it harder for the press to ignore their pronouncements about faith. But it also gave the writers fodder for their columns.

William Myatt wrote tongue-in-cheek about the 1978 phenomenon in a column for the Placerville (California) *Mountain Democrat*:

> *In post-game interview after interview that year, heroes of the day established at the outset that they could take no credit for their accomplishments. They claimed to be playing in the name of a much higher power — every hit, every home run, every spectacular play, every bounce and curve of the ball was attributed directly — to "The Man Upstairs."*
>
> *. . . One local columnist suggested (especially after the Giants' fortune took a turn for the worse) that the players would have a better chance of winning if they concentrated more on the fundamentals of baseball and less on the fundamentals of religion. Another fellow wondered how a particular born-again Giants' outfielder had managed to find God when he hadn't found a cut-off man in five years.*
>
> *. . . verily, I saw the light. I became convinced, based on much eyewitness testimony, that God does indeed roam the diamond like a roving fielder, busting fastballs inside on enemy power hitters and guiding hits into the gap for extra bases. I became further convinced of an even more wonderful truth: God takes sides. And for five months of the 1978 season, God was a Giants' fan.*[45]

Some, like Charles A Fracchia Jr., became lifelong Giants fans beginning in 1978. He described it as a "religious conversion,"[46] not because of the many born-again Giants on the team, but due to the seemingly miraculous nature of the team's run at the pennant.

Were the God Squadders attributing their success on the field to God? If so, was that presumptuous? And where was God when they underperformed? Did the inner peace they discovered make them care less about winning? The press would raise all these questions over the course of the next few years.

Answering those questions requires a deep dive into the God Squad players to better understand their beliefs, motives, and public statements.

Notes

[1] David Bush, "Near Great in 1978/Giants squad brought game back to life in S.F.," *San Francisco Chronicle*, May 31, 2003, C-1.

[2] Dwight Chapin, "Touching Base a Decade Later with Great Giants Staff of '78," *San Francisco Examiner*, June 19, 1998, 27.

[3] Dwight Chapin, "Touching Base a Decade Later with Great Giants Staff of '78," *San Francisco Examiner*, June 19, 1998, 27.

[4] David Bush, "Near Great in 1978/Giants squad brought game back to life in S.F.," *San Francisco Chronicle*, May 31, 2003, C-1.

[5] Bob Stevens, "It's Knepper's Night as Giants Sink Reds, 3-0," *San Francisco Chronicle*, April 22, 1978, 39.

[6] Bob Stevens, "It's Knepper's Night as Giants Sink Reds, 3-0," *San Francisco Chronicle*, April 22, 1978, 39.

[7] Pat Sullivan, "Halicki Readies for '78 Debut," *San Francisco Chronicle*, May 11, 1978, 64.

[8] Leonard Koppett, "Giants are Winning Race in the Bay Area," *The New York Times*, May 23, 1978, C14.

[9] Associated Press, "Giants Starting to Look Unbeatable at Home," *San Rafael Independent Journal*, May 27, 1978, 39.

[10] Associated Press, "Giants Starting to Look Unbeatable at Home," *San Rafael Independent Journal*, May 27, 1978, 39.

[11] Raymond Mungo, "It Was a Great Year for Baseball," *Eureka Times Standard*, October 18, 1978, 19.

[12] Bruce Jenkins, "Just Like Old Days, Except Giants Won," *San Francisco Chronicle*, May 29, 1978, 40.

[13] Lincoln A. Mitchell, *San Francisco Year Zero: Political Upheaval, Punk Rock and a Third-Place Baseball Team* (New Brunswick, NJ: Rutgers University Press, 2020), 92.

[14] Frank Blackman, "Baseball's Giant Comeback," *San Francisco Examiner*, May 29, 1978, 45.

[15] Frank Blackman, "Baseball's Giant Comeback," *San Francisco Examiner*, May 29, 1978, 45.

[16] Larry Keith, "These Giants are Jolly Blue," *Sports Illustrated*, May 29, 1978, 22.

[17] Larry Keith, "These Giants are Jolly Blue," *Sports Illustrated*, May 29, 1978, 22.

[18] Glenn Schwarz, "A Hatful of Heroes," *San Francisco Examiner*, May 30, 1978, 45.

[19] Glenn Schwarz, "Is Knepper Really the NL's Top Lefty?" *San Francisco Examiner*, May 31, 1978, 49.

[20] Herb Caen, "Bay Area Rapid Typewriter," *San Francisco Chronicle*, May 31, 1978, 29.

[21] Stephanie Salter, "Giants' Dream Comes True Again," *San Francisco Examiner*, June 17, 1978, 31.

[22] W.A. Van Winkle, "Look Who's In First," *San Francisco Bay Guardian*, June 25, 1978, 10.

[23] Bill Lyon, "The Giants Get Some Measure of Respect from Philadelphia," *Philadelphia Inquirer*, published in *San Francisco Examiner*, June 30, 1978, 57–58.

[24] Dave Anderson, "Baseball's New Name: Jack Clark," *The New York Times*, July 11, 1978, B14.

[25] Bob Stevens, "Ivie's Pinch Homer Wins It for Blue," *San Francisco Chronicle*, July 26, 1978, 55.

[26] Bob Stevens, "Ivie's Pinch Homer Wins It for Blue," *San Francisco Chronicle*, July 26, 1978, 55.

[27] Joe Sargis, " 'Born-again' Jack Clark Sparks Giants Revival,"

Binghamton Press and Sun-Bulletin, July 29, 1978, 8-C.

[28] Associated Press, "Giants Alone in 1st After Sweep," *The San Bernardino County Sun*, July 31, 1978, 20.

[29] Ron Fimrite, "Going Flat Out in California Before Howling Crowds in Candlestick Park, Those Two Bitter Rivals, the Giants and the Dodgers, Split a Rousing Four-Game Series in a Vain Attempt to Determine Who Was the Best in the West," *Sports Illustrated*, August 14, 1978, 20.

[30] Ron Fimrite, "Going Flat Out in California Before Howling Crowds in Candlestick Park, Those Two Bitter Rivals, the Giants and the Dodgers, Split a Rousing Four-Game Series in a Vain Attempt to Determine Who Was the Best in the West," *Sports Illustrated*, August 14, 1978, 20.

[31] Ron Fimrite, "The Battle is Rejoined with the Giants Contending Again," *Sports Illustrated*, August 7, 1978, 30.

[32] Anonymous, "Giants and Dodgers Tangle Again in California: An Old Rivalry Gets a New Lease on Life," *Time*, August 28, 1978, 62.

[33] Anonymous, "Giants and Dodgers Tangle Again in California: An Old Rivalry Gets a New Lease on Life," *Time*, August 28, 1978, 62.

[34] Glenn Schwarz, "Down for the Count, But Not Out," *San Francisco Examiner*, August 14, 1978, 49.

[35] Glenn Schwarz, "Down for the Count, But Not Out," *San Francisco Examiner*, August 14, 1978, 50.

[36] Jim Kaplan, "The Week (August 13-19)," *Sports Illustrated*, August 28, 1978, 78.

[37] Dwight Chapin, "Touching Base a Decade Later with Great Giants Staff of '78," *San Francisco Examiner*, June 19, 1998, 34.

[38] Glenn Dickey, *San Francisco Giants 40 Years* (San Francisco: Woodford Press, 1997), 95, 99.

[39] Dwight Chapin, "Touching Base a Decade Later with Great Giants Staff of '78," *San Francisco Examiner*, June 19, 1998, 34.

[40] David Bush, "Near Great in 1978/Giants squad brought game back to life in S.F.," *San Francisco Chronicle*, May 31, 2003, C-1.

[41] David Bush, "Near Great in 1978/Giants squad brought game back to life in S.F.," *San Francisco Chronicle*, May 31, 2003, C-1.

[42] Dwight Chapin, "Touching Base a Decade Later with Great Giants Staff of '78," *San Francisco Examiner*, June 19, 1998, 34.

[43] Glenn Schwarz, "How Giants Turned On, Tuned In and Dropped Out of Pennant Race," *San Francisco Examiner*, September 26, 1978, 45.

[44] Glenn Schwarz, "How Giants Turned On, Tuned In and Dropped Out of Pennant Race," *San Francisco Examiner*, September 26, 1978, 45.

[45] William Myatt, "The Ultimate Free Agent," *Mountain Democrat*, September 2, 1981, 60.

[46] Lincoln A. Mitchell, *San Francisco Year Zero: Political Upheaval, Punk Rock and a Third-Place Baseball Team* (New Brunswick, NJ: Rutgers University Press, 2020), 247.

Chapter 3
The Lieutenant

In Cohn's controversial column (is that redundant?) entitled "Lavelle and the Fiend," discussed in chapter thirteen of this book, he referred to the pitcher as the lieutenant of the God Squad. That's because Lavelle played an important role in several of his teammates becoming born-again Christians. He had become a believer a couple of years before the born-again boom of the Giants in 1978.

Raised in Bethlehem, Pennsylvania, Lavelle grew up playing football, basketball, and baseball, but the latter was his first love. He pitched a couple of no-hitters in high school, was drafted by the Giants after he graduated, and spent eight seasons in the minors as a starting pitcher. But he almost quit baseball. Lavelle recalled:

> *I was beginning to think I'd never get a shot with the big club. I was with Phoenix three years and kept noticing the Giants often didn't have a left-handed reliever. That gave me hope. Yet every spring they sent me down. I was seriously considering retiring. Then somebody spoke up for me. I think it was Andy Gilbert, then a coach with the Giants. I had pitched for Andy when he managed Amarillo of the Texas League. When San Francisco called me up in September 1974, I was very surprised.*[1]

He didn't disappoint. He relieved in ten late-season

games for a total of seventeen innings with a 2.12 ERA. As a rookie in 1975, he pitched in sixty-five games, posting a 6–3 record with a 2.95 ERA and eight saves. After spring training in 1976, manager Bill Rigney made Lavelle what is now termed the "closer." He went 10–6 that season with a 2.69 ERA and twelve saves.

In 1977 he had a 2.05 ERA with twenty saves and was selected to the National League All-Star team by Cincinnati Reds manager Sparky Anderson. The *Examiner* wrote:

> *"I didn't know for sure I would be going. But I was hoping," Lavelle said. "Sparky told me when we were in Cincinnati that I was heavy on his mind. He said he had to make a lot of hard decisions, but that I shouldn't get discouraged because I was still high on his list. I'm really grateful. And I just thank the Lord I'm on that team. I didn't set it as a goal this year, but it's always in the back of your mind when you play. My main goal is to be on a world championship team."*[2]

That last wish never came true, but Lavelle had a fine career. The southpaw reliever pitched with the Giants for eleven seasons and is fourth in all-time saves for the club, with 126. He is also number one on the club in games finished, with 369, and in games pitched, 647, more than Hall of Famer Christy Mathewson, in second place with 635. Lavelle was traded to the Toronto Blue Jays in 1985 and retired as an Oakland A in 1987. His lifetime ERA is 2.93.

Lavelle spoke about his relief role.

"I really do enjoy (the role)," he said. "You have to stay in every game mentally, because you never know whether you'll be in the game for real or not. One thing I really like is that I don't have to sit around three or four days fretting about that next scheduled start."[3]

He married in 1972, and he and his wife, Regina, had their first child, daughter Jana, in 1975.

"I'd fulfilled a dream," said Lavelle. "I had success, money, a beautiful wife, our first child . . . but there was something missing."[4]

He told the *San Francisco Examiner* in 1977:

> *There's a time in each person's life when he asks why he's here and what he's doing. I went searching when I was 26 and playing winter ball in Maracay, Venezuela, in November of '75. That's when I met a Christian brother, Tom Johnson, who now pitches for the Minnesota Twins.*
>
> *He told me about his personal relationship with Jesus. He had a peace of mind about him, and I decided I wanted to have it. He told me to accept Jesus Christ as my Lord and savior, to put him in charge of things. Well, I did accept him. He came in and took control of things and, wow . . .*
>
> *I was searching for something to grasp onto. There was a void within me. I was a pessimist, worried a lot and didn't have peace of mind. He said He would come into my life and He has.*[5]

He told this author, "It was an inner peace I had, that I felt God was the one who gave me the talent to play and I wanted to use it for His glory. And I had just the peace about doing the best that I could do. I think God calls us to whatever we put our hand to, to do with all our heart. And that's what I tried to do."[6]

His transformation baffled reporters. They were used to the old Gary who would angrily vent his frustration after a poor performance.

"I asked the Lord for strength and before long the press began to report on my new-found composure," Lavelle recalled.[7]

His teammates also noticed the change, and when opportunities arose, Lavelle told them about his relationship with Jesus. Although one author wrote that when Lavelle came to spring training in 1976 he was the only professing Christian on the ballclub,[8] the pitcher is not so certain.

"I don't know," said Lavelle. "Everybody has a different take on what a Christian is. I would say I knew I was born again and I approached it that way. There might have been other guys who were just not outgoing about it, but believed."[9]

Lavelle shared his faith with his teammates whenever the opportunity presented itself.

"A lot of guys observe your lifestyle," said the southpaw. "They look at that from the standpoint of, 'Is this guy a hypocrite or is this guy the real deal?' So I tried to live my life in a way that was pleasing to the Lord, and if guys saw that, we would get into discussions at times in various ways. I think what helped was we had Bible studies [usually in Lavelle's home] with Lloyd [Mashore, chaplain to the Giants], and that really allowed for guys to be prayed for and witnessed to and then they would make those commitments."[10]

Lavelle said that his newfound faith did not alter how he tackled his job.

"I don't think there was a different approach," he said. "I always had a very competitive attitude in everything, particularly in baseball."[11]

Coming out of the bullpen in the late innings was Lavelle's specialty, but he hit a rough patch in 1978. Then, after a stellar performance in early July in which he gave up just one hit in 3 2/3 innings and got the win against the Cincinnati Reds, he was quick to thank God and his teammate.

"It's been a struggle for me and I just want to thank Jesus for showing me that I haven't been aggressive enough." he said. "When I went out there in the seventh inning, [catcher] Marc Hill told me he wanted me going after the hitters. After that, my ball took off. It had added velocity."[12]

But his biggest challenge came in 1980.

"I'd gotten off to a terrible start and lost my job as the number one reliever [to Al Holland]," he shared. "I kept asking the Lord, 'Is this the end of my career?'"[13]

He started a weight training program the following year, During the winter of 1981, he was anticipating a trade, but manager Frank Robinson showed faith in him in the spring. His arm had returned to form. His 10–7 mark, eight saves, and 2.67 ERA helped keep the Giants in the 1982 pennant race until the next-to-last day of the season.

Again, Lavelle credited God with his comeback.

"He gave me the desire to work hard, to go the extra mile," he said. "I learned to persevere when the odds are against you, but it also made me realize baseball will end someday and I'll need to go on."[14]

The Giants exhibited more trust in Lavelle by trading Holland after the 1982 season to Philadelphia, with Lavelle reclaiming the closer role in 1983.

"I figure to get a lot of work this year with Al [Holland] gone, and that suits me fine," Lavelle said in spring training of 1983. "I would be lying if I said that I enjoyed coming into games in the middle innings or being used as the team's third short reliever. But I also understood Frank Robinson's reasoning. When you have [Greg] Minton and Al pitching as effectively as they did during the past two seasons, you naturally go with them in the tight situations."[15]

Lavelle took advantage of the opportunity, posting a 7–4 mark with a 2.59 ERA and twenty saves in 1983.

As for sharing his faith, Lavelle told the *Examiner* in 1977, "I don't preach. I just share what the Bible has to say about life."[16] He added in a 1983 interview, "I don't regard myself as a fire-and-brimstone preacher who thinks of himself as perfect. I've never even openly preached to players on this team."[17]

Lavelle's low-key approach appeared to win over Robinson when the latter was appointed the new manager of the Giants in 1981.

"I . . . had lunch with Lavelle, who gave me the background on the Born Again Christians," said Robinson. "Look, I don't mind. We had Pat Kelly on the Orioles, who was outspoken, and Scott McGregor, who was quiet about it. I just told him that I don't want interference with what I'm trying to do with the club and the clubhouse, and he said fine."[18]

When the Giants were close to trading Lavelle to the California Angels in 1985 (the deal fell through, and Lavelle was dealt instead to the Toronto Blue Jays), Art Rosenbaum wrote in the *Chronicle*:

> *Lavelle will also fit well in the Angels' uniform. This year, celebrating the club's 25th year in the American League, a new logo shows the letter "A" with a halo circling the point of the "A." It's only symbolic, of course, but Lavelle's sincerity in his search for converts cannot be questioned. His home has been a gathering place for athletes of deepest*

Christian faith. For a time he displayed a rack of religious literature in his locker at Candlestick Park until an adviser—not the Giants' front office or manager—persuaded him it was becoming controversial. In any case, Lavelle and a halo go together.[19]

Notes

[1] Pat Frizzell, "Giants' Reliever Succeeds Where Others Fail," *Oakland Tribune*, May 7, 1976, 47.

[2] Glenn Schwarz, "A Rewarding Day for Giants," *San Francisco Examiner*, July 14, 1977, 58.

[3] Ted Meixell, "Lavelle Feels He's Entering his Prime," *The Morning Call*, May 6, 1981, 110.

[4] Matt Sieger, "Bullpen, Bars, Bible," *Sharing the Victory*, July/August 1983, 9.

[5] Glenn Schwarz, "Lavelle and the Lord," *San Francisco Examiner*, May 29, 1977, 33.

[6] Gary Lavelle, interview with author, June 1, 2023.

[7] Glenn Schwarz, "Lavelle and the Lord," *San Francisco Examiner*, May 29, 1977, 33.

[8] Duane Sandul, *When Faith Steals Home* (Plainfield, NJ: Logos International, 1980), 96.

[9] Gary Lavelle, interview with author, June 1, 2023.

[10] Gary Lavelle, interview with author, June 1, 2023.

[11] Gary Lavelle, interview with author, June 1, 2023.

[12] Glenn Schwarz, "Lavelle Shuts off the Reds' Lights," *San Francisco Examiner*, July 9, 1978, 31.

[13] Matt Sieger, "Bullpen, Bars, Bible," *Sharing the Victory*, July/August 1983, 9.

[14] Matt Sieger, "Bullpen, Bars, Bible," *Sharing the Victory*, July/August 1983, 9.

[15] Fred Guzman, "With Holland Gone, Lavelle Won't Be Left Out

this Year," *San Jose Mercury*, March 28, 1983, 78.

[16] Glenn Schwarz, "Lavelle and the Lord," *San Francisco Examiner*, May 29, 1977, 33.

[17] Fred Guzman, "With Holland Gone, Lavelle Won't Be Left Out this Year," *San Jose Mercury*, March 28, 1983, 81.

[18] Peter Gammons, "Lord, Please Bless F. Robby," *The Boston Globe*, published in *The Fresno Bee*, February 22, 1981, 80.

[19] Art Rosenbaum, "Will the Giants' Lavelle Be an Angel in '85?" *San Francisco Chronicle*, January 10, 1985, 68.

Chapter 4
Bob Knepper

After his senior year at Calistoga (California) High, Knepper was selected by the Giants in the second round of the 1972 free-agent draft.

"I got a lot of support from my parents," said Knepper, "My mother always said I would pitch for the Giants. My father took a lot of heat for letting me pass up college to play ball."[1]

At 6'2", 195 pounds, Knepper threw a 94-mph fastball. With the Triple A Fresno Giants in 1974, he went 20–5 and struck out 247 in 239 innings, the best performance by a California League pitcher in thirteen seasons.

At age twenty-two, Knepper made his first major league start with the Giants on September 10, 1976, then had a decent rookie season in 1977, going 11-9 with a 3.36 ERA for a team that went 71–91.

His breakthrough season was 1978, with a 17–11 mark and a 2.63 ERA. It also happened to be the season he became a born–again Christian.

Knepper told this author how that came about:

I pretty much considered myself an atheist by the time I arrived in the big leagues at the end of 1976. Getting to the big leagues put me as a teammate of Gary Lavelle's. So we struck up a friendship and I began talking with him about Christ . . . debating really. I found Gary to be the first person who had a relationship with Christ vs. a shallow belief like most "Christians."

As the '76 and '77 seasons came and went, Gary proved to be a tough nut to crack. He had answers for my questions that other Christians didn't have and he had questions I couldn't answer.

In spring training of 1978 I happened to get trapped in the locker room during a chapel service where the speaker, Jimmy Mammou, gave his testimony. His testimony simply blew me away. But not enough to change any of my thoughts.

Then in April we were in San Diego and Jimmy was the speaker for the chapel service again. I cannot remember ever having the same speaker twice in one year, let alone in two different cities. This time after Jimmy's talk, I was impressed enough to ask Gary if he would help me study the Bible, primarily because in his testimony, Jimmy said the Bible promises that if you earnestly seek God, there is a promise that you will find Him.

So I reasoned that I would "search" earnestly for God, and I would either find Him—good—or I wouldn't find Him, which would prove that the Bible was a lie and I would be off the hook. My whole motivation has always been to find the truth, and even as an atheist, I wanted to know the truth.

During this time, Gary gave me a book by Hal Lindsey which stated that many theologians believed Christ would return in our lifetime. I knew that if that were true and He came back, I would be headed south [hell] vs. north [heaven]. Also around these times, my grandmother's house blew up from a faulty gas valve, killing her. She was the first person close to me that died, so some questions about *life and death were floating around in my mind.*

On the night of my first game in the major leagues in 1976, my dad suffered a heart attack and almost died. So, God was working in my life even though I was unaware. Also, while I was having a great season in 1978, I wasn't finding the fulfillment I thought I would.

With all that was going on in my life, I finally came to the point one night in my hotel room where I asked God to reveal Himself to me and come into my life as my Lord and Savior. As I lay in my bed praying, I began weeping with great wracking sobs as I poured my heart out to Him.

I explain it as me coming face to face with the sinfulness of Bob Knepper and the holiness of God. I must have cried with huge sobs of brokenness for twenty to thirty minutes. When I finished, His peace that passes all understanding settled into my heart and I knew as a baby Christian that I had been forgiven and accepted.[2]

1979 was a tough year for the Giants and Knepper.

"When we finished third in 1978, Bob put too much pressure on himself [the next season]," Lavelle told *Sports Illustrated's* Jim Kaplan.[3]

Knepper agreed, telling Kaplan, "In 1977 and 1978 Herm Starrette was our pitching coach. He told me, 'If you don't have good stuff, you're still better than a lot of other guys, so just go out there and pitch.' When Herm left in 1979, I didn't concentrate on the hitter and thought about outside problems. I was throwing too hard."[4]

He told the *Examiner*, "Shep (Larry Shepard, then the Giants pitching coach) didn't know me or my style so he wasn't sure what I was doing. But I started looking for things, and by May I had myself a sore arm. I had myself into a hole and I kept digging it deeper . . . I was always looking for something to improve my windup or a particular pitch, and I wasn't concentrating on the hitters." [5]

Knepper slipped to 9–12 in 1979 with a 4.64 ERA. Midseason, Shepard said, "He's such a believer in being a form pitcher, a picture pitcher. He's searching. He concerns himself more with form rather than playing hard baseball. He's looking for that flow. But you can't make it simple. Pitching is contrary to the human body."[6]

His pitching was again subpar in 1980, as he lost sixteen games against nine wins, with a 4.10 ERA.

"He was falling behind hitters and they were waiting for his fastball," said Giants third baseman Darrell Evans.[7]

After Knepper was traded to the Astros following the 1980 season, Vida Blue said, "When he was over here [with the Giants], he would get two strikes on a batter and then, maybe, he would lose him on four straight balls. He would agonize over that last batter instead of worrying about the next one. He'd obviously be rattled. And then he'd start thinking—'What should I do? What should I do?' Then he'd get into more trouble after that."[8]

Knepper had the same opinion, telling the *Oakland Tribune* in early June 1979, "Concentration is a problem for me, no doubt. I'm always looking for the perfect pitch or the perfect delivery. Then I start trying too hard, and it just gets worse."[9]

Knepper pointed to other reasons.

"It's so difficult to put a handle on it," he told Art Rosenbaum of the *Chronicle*. "Various factors kept me off balance, so to speak. There was so much misinterpretation about my religious beliefs . . . Maybe it's the morality of the community, but some people didn't seem to want to understand, to permit me my freedom of choice. I never want to have to apologize for believing in God. Never."[10]

In April 1981, as his first season with the Astros got underway, he told Stan Vaughn of the *Napa Valley* Register:

> *Before the trade to Houston, I questioned whether I wanted to play ball anymore. It got so bad last year I didn't like going to the ballpark. I usually look forward to spring training, but I was dreading this year [before the Giants traded him to the Astros in December 1980]. I just didn't enjoy being in that locker room. I didn't have freedom of religion, or almost freedom of speech.*[11]

Vaughn wrote:

> *When the media got more personal in its diatribes of the Christians on the team, Knepper grew less talkative. "It got to the point where the worst part of my day was talking to the press. I was figuring out ways to avoid them this season. The press holds a lot of power, and it's a responsibility they have to realize. They don't have to write a complimentary article all the time, but they don't have to be abusive either."*[12]

Knepper told Jill Lieber of *Sports Illustrated*, "The press and the Bay Area fans really tore into me. The criticism came so fast and hit me so hard that I couldn't cope. I retreated within myself. I quit being outgoing and aggressive."[13]

John Lindblom of *The Mercury News* wrote in September 1981:

> *Much of Knepper's unhappiness as a Giant stemmed from the media. He said he quit reading the newspapers after the*

'78 season. He said his main concern was how the publicity affected his family.

"It was easier for me to take than it was for my family and friends," said Knepper. "It's really tough to see how it affects them. People on talk shows were saying I was spending more time reading the Bible than I was worrying about my pitching. My mom heard Ken Dito on his radio show say that 'Knepper is through and they ought to give Montefusco a chance.'

"That didn't bother me too much because I don't think Ken Dito is necessarily the smartest guy in baseball. But he's not going to judge my career and when he did he hurt my mom."[14]

Knepper was resuscitated on the mound in Houston, going 9–5 with a 2.18 ERA in the strike-shortened 1981 season and making the All-Star team. The new surroundings with the Astros suited him.

Knepper noted:

...everything was great in 1978, but when everybody started to point the finger at each other in 1979, I wasn't ready for that. I wasn't mature enough to handle all the negative reaction that all the Christians on the team were getting. The Bay Area is a liberal area, anyway, with an anti-Christian atmosphere, so it was good for me to leave at the time that I did [1981]. I went down to Houston, which is down in the Bible Belt, and it gave me time to recover and to get the spiritual growth that I needed.[15]

As Rosenbaum wrote in August 1981, "Knepper is no longer disturbed by snickering references to his membership on the Giants' noted 'God Squad,' a collection of praying players. Aside from his right to his own beliefs, he never understood why his own inner-self should have been constantly lined up with the way his curve ball did, or did not, dance."[16]

Knepper told Stan Hochman of the *Philadelphia Daily News* in October 1981, when the Astros were playing the Los Angeles Dodgers in the National League Division Series:

> *Pitch in San Francisco, that's the toughest mental exercise I know. Theoretically, you should not allow weather [Candlestick Park's notorious fog and cold winds] or anything you can't control, affect you. That's theoretical. Few people can play in that type of ballpark, with an organization that has problems, with a low-quality media dragging you down.*
>
> *The ballpark is bleak, the field is bad, the organization is a joke, the Bay area media is lousy. So you come to a place where the weather is nice, even when it's raining outside, a super ballpark with fans who support you, and a front office trying to help you play better. My experiences here in Houston are what I dreamed that major-league baseball was supposed to be like. Fun, excitement.*[17]

"I'm happy," Knepper said to Rosenbaum, "because of the general attitude of the organization. I'm allowed to do and believe as I choose. I feel I'm respected for myself as well as for what I might accomplish on the mound. Another thing—I love the Astrodome. It's a pitcher's park."[18]

But, as we shall see, Knepper would have troubles in Houston as well—not because of his faith, but in part because of his tendency to think too much.

As Tom Halliburton wrote in 1988 in the *Port Arthur* (Texas) *News*:

> *Perhaps more than any player I've ever met, Bob Knepper is cut out to be a sports writer. He reads constantly. He overanalyzes everything. He's very opinionated. He's quiet by nature but his opinions travel the world because he's a public figure.*
>
> "The rest of us analyze something once," [Houston Astros' teammate] Bill Doran said. "Bob analyzes things four and five times."
>
> That's why it's easy to call Knepper a head case whenever his pitching performances turn sour. Sure enough, his mind has admittedly played a role in Knepper's mound struggles.[19]

Notes

[1] Jim Kaplan, "Resurrection in Houston," *Sports Illustrated*, September 21, 1981, 51.

[2] Bob Knepper, interview with author, June 18, 2023.

[3] Jim Kaplan, "Resurrection in Houston," *Sports Illustrated*, September 21, 1981, 51.

[4] Jim Kaplan, "Resurrection in Houston," *Sports Illustrated*, September 21, 1981, 51.

[5] Stephanie Salter, "The Quintessential Bob Knepper," *San Francisco Examiner*, May 25, 1980, 271.

[6] Ralph Wiley, "Knepper Lacks in Concentration," *Oakland Tribune*, July 5, 1979, 53.

[7] Jim Kaplan, "Resurrection in Houston," *Sports Illustrated*, September 21, 1981, 46.

[8] Terence Moore, "Knepper Has Found Peace of Mind," *San

Francisco Examiner, August 12, 1981, 65.

[9] Ralph Wiley, "Knepper Lacks in Concentration," *Oakland Tribune*, July 5, 1979, 53.

[10] Art Rosenbaum, "A Happy Astro," *San Francisco Chronicle*, August 12, 1981, 63.

[11] Stan Vaughn, "Faith Leads Knepper, Hubbard in Pro Sports Maze," *Napa Valley Register*, April 18, 1981, 6.

[12] Stan Vaughn, "Faith Leads Knepper, Hubbard in Pro Sports Maze," *Napa Valley Register*, April 18, 1981, 8.

[13] Jill Lieber, "Some Say No Leica: Bob Knepper Has a Decidedly Controversial Focus on the World, But His Pitching this Year is Right on Target," *Sports Illustrated*, June 20, 1988, 50.

[14] John Lindblom, "A Heck of a Good Season for Knepper in Houston," *Sunday Mercury News*, September 13, 1981, 53.

[15] Terence Moore, "Baseball and Religion," *Atlanta Journal-Constitution*, August 13,1989, C-1.

[16] Art Rosenbaum, "A Happy Astro," *San Francisco Chronicle*, August 12, 1981, 59.

[17] Stan Hochman, "Knepper Thankful Home is Dome," *Philadelphia Daily News*, October 9, 1981, 122.

[18] Art Rosenbaum, "A Happy Astro," *San Francisco Chronicle*, August 12, 1981, 59.

[19] Tom Halliburton, "Knepper's Hard Work Does Not Go Unrewarded," *Port Arthur News,* July 10, 1988, 10.

Chapter 5
Rob Andrews

Andrews, the brother of Mike Andrews, also a major leaguer, played his first two seasons for the Houston Astros before they traded hm to the Giants during spring training of 1977. The Giants released him after the end of the 1979 season, which marked the end of his major league career.

While he had over four hundred at-bats in both 1976 and 1977, he was not an everyday starter at Houston and was utilized primarily as a utility infielder by the Giants in 1978 and 1979, logging only 177 and 154 at-bats, respectively, In August 1979, he told *Chronicle* columnist Rosenbaum that he wanted to play every day or be traded to a team where he could do so. If that didn't work out, he was preparing to become a minister.

Andrews shared with Rosenbaum a copy of a pamphlet that he kept by his locker. Rosenbaum related:

In his pamphlet Andrews tells how he was saved... how "I gave my baseball career to God and told Him I trusted in His will for me."

... Andrews then explains how all the goodies — money, fame, girls and good times — did not bring happiness. One night in Philadelphia the pressure within him caused an explosion. He was playing poorly and was so upset he walked off the field between innings and packed his bags. He

realized, looking in the mirror, that he was trying to take on the whole world by himself . . . instinctively, he asked for God's help.

God answered, he saw, by sending him to the Giants where he met Lavelle and a local pastor, Lloyd Mashore, who helped him understand more about God's control of life, and eventually a commitment from which "I would experience true, genuine happiness . . . (after) surrendering my baseball career to God."[1]

In a July 1978 interview, Andrews talked about how his faith helped him handle his backup role on the Giants:

I've been a starter all my career, and if I hadn't become a Christian, I never would have been able to handle the situation. Now I can emulate Jesus and give 100 percent of myself if it means sitting on the bench or pitching batting practice. I used to be a hell-raiser. I'd go into bars and tear them apart, get into fights, hang out with all the cowboys and stuff like that before I realized there is a purpose in life. Society tells you all along that you're the cream of the crop, and everybody looks up to you, and suddenly you have a large pride and ego, and that old macho image—be a man and do it yourself. The Lord had to lower me down about 20 notches before he could even work in my life, and I'm thankful he did.[2]

Released by the Giants after the 1979 season, Andrews tried out with the Mets in the spring of 1980. It looked as if he had landed a spot as a utility infielder until he suffered injuries to his back and arm. The Mets wanted to send him to the minors until he recovered.[3]

That's when, at age twenty-seven, he decided to retire.

"I was just a little frustrated with sitting on the bench in San Francisco and not once having the chance to play regularly in my whole career," Andrews told Alan Arakelian of the *Santa Cruz* (California) *Sentinel*. "I didn't feel like sitting on the bench in Shea Stadium (in New York). I kind of made a covenant to the Lord, that if I had to go down to the minors, I would hang it up."[4]

After Andrews retired from baseball and was working as a youth pastor and teacher, George Vecsey of *The New York Times* interviewed him for a May 1981 article about religion in baseball. Andrews said, "I saw Gary Lavelle go through hard times that would have killed me. But he was always calm. He never preached to me but one day I asked him, 'Gary, what is it?' He said it was Christ."[5]

So Andrews was yet another Giant who Lavelle helped come to faith in Jesus. At least one person noticed the difference—Andrews' manager in late 1979, Dave Bristol.

"I saw Rob Andrews turn his life around, and that was great," said Bristol.[6]

Andrews told the *Santa Cruz Sentinel*, "I was Rob Andrews, the baseball player. When I became a Christian (in 1978), I didn't have any need for any artificial stimulation for my ego."[7]

Andrews was not afraid to proclaim his newfound beliefs while with the Giants. When he autographed the pamphlet with his photograph that he gave Rosenbaum, he scribbled below it Romans 1:16. That verse in the New Testament reads, "For I am not ashamed of the gospel, for it is the power of God for salvation to everyone who believes, to the Jew first and also to the Greek."[8]

Andrews showed he was not ashamed after a nationally

televised game in St. Louis on July 17, 1978, when he beat the Cardinals with a ninth-inning home run. It was his first major-league home run in 1,228 at-bats and his second game-winning hit in three days. In the post-game television interview, he shared his faith in Jesus.

"The Lord is a great stagesetter," he later told the *San Francisco Examiner* about that day. "It gave me the opportunity to share my testimony with millions of people. I think God is using the Giants this year, the way he used the Denver Broncos [football team] last year to bring glory to his name. I think he's using athletics to bring faith out of the closet. There are 24 men on our roster, and we can reach millions."[9]

Being his first, the home run was a big deal for Andrews. *The St. Louis Post-Dispatch* reported:

> *"I was looking for a fastball and he threw me a slider. I didn't think the ball would go out of the park. I saw it hooking and expected it to fall in somewhere. I thought I just might try for second. I was digging for second when I looked up to see where the ball was. It was a struggle to make all the bases. I was on Cloud 9."*
>
> *Andrews said that after he arrived in the dugout he asked his teammates to verify whether he had touched all the bases.*
>
> *"I think five or six guys passed out on the bench after I hit the homer," Andrews said. "I was stunned. I thought, 'What's going on here?' Then I saw the umpire motioning me around. When you haven't hit a homer in 1,200 and some at-bats, you just don't get much chance to practice trotting around the bases."*
>
> *. . . Said Andrews with a big sigh, "It's definitely the*

highlight of my career. I still can't believe the ball went over the fence."[10]

The ball actually hit the top of the left-field fence and hopped over. Andrews said, "I honestly believe God picked that ball up and carried it over the fence."[11]

Teammate Darrell Evans wouldn't go that far, but said, "I'm not going to say we're a team of destiny. But we sure win games in the strangest ways."[12]

Notes

[1] Art Rosenbaum, "The Lord and Rob Andrews," *San Francisco Chronicle*, August 28, 1979, 50.

[2] Albert Morch, "God and the Giants," *San Francisco Examiner*, July 31, 1978, 21.

[3] John Kawamoto, "Ex-Giant Rob Andrews Reborn as Youth Pastor," *San Francisco Examiner*, April 22, 1981, 75.

[4] Alan Arakelian, "Ex-Giant: There's More to Life than Baseball," *Santa Cruz Sentinel*, May 20, 1982, 51.

[5] George Vecsey, "Religion Becomes an Important Part of Baseball Scene," *The New York Times*, May 10, 1981, section 5, 1.

[6] George Vecsey, "Religion Becomes an Important Part of Baseball Scene," *The New York Times*, May 10, 1981, section 5, 1.

[7] Alan Arakelian, "Ex-Giant: There's More to Life than Baseball," *Santa Cruz Sentinel*, May 20, 1982, 51.

[8] Romans 1:16, New American Standard Bible.

[9] Albert Morch, "God and the Giants," *San Francisco Examiner*, July 31, 1978, 21.

[10] Neil Russo, "One in 1200 Homer Beats Cards," *St. Louis Post-Dispatch*, July 18, 1978, 10-A.

[11] Morris H. Rubin, "Of All Things," *The Capital Times*, January 29, 1979, 20.

[12] Glenn Schwarz, "Andrews Applauded by Giants," *San Francisco Examiner*, July 18, 1978, 41.

Chapter 6
Jack Clark

Whitey Herzog, who managed Clark when he played for the St. Louis Cardinals from 1985 to 1987, called him "the greatest fastball hitter of our era."[1] In his eighteen-year career, the right-handed slugger, dubbed "Jack the Ripper" by Vida Blue, belted 340 home runs and drove in 1,180 runs. He won the Silver Slugger Award in 1985 and 1987.

The Giants signed Clark as a thirteenth-round draft pick after he graduated high school. A standout high school pitcher, he got hit hard in the Giants' Pioneer Rookie League in Great Falls, Montana, in 1973. He was moved to the outfield and hit .321 with fifty-four RBIs in sixty-five games.

His next stop was the Arizona Instructional League, where he led the winter league with a .363 batting average and was converted to a third baseman.

"He wasn't a bad third baseman," recalled Knepper, his teammate in the minors. "But when we were at Fresno, there was talk of giving the fans behind first base gloves for their protection."[2]

Clark reported to spring training in 1976 hoping to make the big club, but the Giants acquired Ken Reitz from the Cardinals to play third base. So Clark was optioned to Phoenix where he played the outfield and batted .323 with twenty-nine doubles, sixteen triples, and seventeen homers for a .562 slugging percentage.

He hit .321 in spring training the next season and made the major league club but was platooned much of his rookie year. Frustrated that he was not a regular starter, he rebelled, sometimes not running out ground balls.

"It was my toughest year in baseball," said Clark. "I wasn't hustling and people got on my can. It bothered me a lot. I was wrong, but I wanted to be defiant, to show the Giants I didn't like being treated that way. It was as if the club was telling me, 'You're 21 and you should be happy to be in the bigs.' Well, that was a bunch of bull. I was here because I wanted to play and I had earned it."[3]

In the midst of his frustration, he spoke with Lavelle about spiritual matters and began to attend the Giants' Baseball Chapel meetings.

"It relaxed me," Clark said. "I could see the Lord blessing my life. I'm not a Jesus freak but I have inner peace."[4]

His breakout year was 1978, both in attitude and performance. He was selected to the All-Star team for the first of four times.

"I don't think Jack gave 110 percent last year," said Giants relief pitcher Greg Minton in 1978. "He couldn't accept the platooning and it got to him. Now his mind has caught up to his body. The game is important to him and so are his teammates. He knows he can't stay up and party every night. Jack has a much better sense of priorities now. He seems to be working a lot harder."[5]

Clark elaborated on his faith to the *San Francisco Examiner* in July 1978:

> *It's not religion we're into here, it has more to do with faith. It was a year ago, about this time, that I was reborn. I got talking to some people. I bought my first Bible and read a*

> little bit out of it each day — and my spirit began to grow.
>
> . . . I'm proud to be on a team with Christian ballplayers and be able to share the Lord with them. It has given me a peace of mind I've never had before. If you don't know how to handle it, the game can really get to you . . .
>
> I've given it all to the Lord, I give him credit for my victories and defeats, and I know there's gonna be more defeats than victories. Earlier this season, I had a hitting streak that ended at 19. I started all over again and now it's up to 26. If that streak ended today, and I went 0-for-4 today, I'd give the 0-for-4 to the Lord, and thank him for giving me the chance to be out here at all.[6]

Clark got the chance to thank the Lord. He went 0-for-4 that day.

John B. Koffend of *Us* magazine profiled Clark in August 1978, writing, "Only last year, his first full season with the Giants, Clark sassed the umps, threw his bat an angry mile after fanning at the plate, gave the finger to hecklers and was thumbed out of several games. But not this season. Now the heckler may get the finger, but it points to heaven like a prophet's — Jack Clark's way of identifying the source of all things."[7]

Koffend closed his article this way: "Says a Giant trainer bluntly: 'Last year Jack Clark was an asshole. This year he's playing ball the way it should be played. I don't know if Christianity did it, but something did it.'"[8]

UPI sportswriter Joe Sargis wrote in July 1978 about Clark's transformation:

> Clark, who has batted .300 consistently all season long and played in this year's All-Star game, was a moody young

man a year ago. Often, when he failed to get a hit in a key spot, he would sulk or throw a bat. Off the field, he seemed lost and bewildered. Twice manager Joe Altobelli had to fine him for being late to practice.

Then a big transformation took place last spring [actually later in the 1977 season] when Clark made the commitment to become a born-again Christian.

"Everything changed overnight for me," Clark recalls. "Instead of seeing the dark side of things I became a lot more tolerant, not only of others, but myself as well. I can't begin to tell you what becoming a Christian has done for me, but I'm not the preaching type. I leave that to others who have better vocabularies and know how to talk to people about making a commitment. I'm happy to leave everything in the Lord's hands and go from there."[9]

He may not have preached, but Clark was not shy about declaring his newfound faith. Bob Slocum of *The Modesto (California) Bee* wrote in August 1978:

Clark is another who uses the public airways to exult his born-again emergence. A sulker and malcontent last season when he was platooned, Clark has been among the National League's top batting, home run and RBI leaders all season and unashamedly credits his transformation to his newfound faith in Christ. During All-Star Game introductions last month, Clark stepped forward and raised his index finger to indicate, "He is the One."[10]

He may have been a bit overzealous. Sportswriter Emery Filmer observed:

> Clark may have overstepped his bounds by persuading teammates into the same beliefs. Some jumped aboard as the Giants were accordingly referred to as the "God Squad." But several players didn't exactly warm up to his ad campaign.
>
> "Jack has always meant well but he may have tried too hard with some guys," LeMaster said. "Now, I think, he has stopped trying to change the world. He's working for himself and it's starting to pay off."[11]

Working for himself included setting boundaries off the field.

"Everybody's different," he said. "Some guys stay out all night drinkin' and chasin' women. I can't do it that way. You have to have a spiritual life, in order to take something home from the ballpark."[12]

The *Santa Cruz Sentinel* wrote this about Clark in July 1979:

> Late in his rookie season [1977], Clark became a born-again Christian — and it has influenced his life ever since.
>
> "My faith keeps me at the one level I need to be at in the game, which is probably where I'm maturing more in my career and life," said Clark, who was a National League All-Star last season. "Where I'm living up to my potential is with the Lord.
>
> "I just stay at that level and give all the glory and the agony to the Lord," he said. "He blesses my life that way. I feel I've got more peace of mind than ever before right now. God is more important in my life than baseball will ever be. He's No. 1 in my life. Baseball is second."[13]

In his *San Francisco Chronicle* column early in the 1981 season, Glenn Dickey took a poke at Clark's faith:

> *Jack Clark continues to be an enigma for the Giants. His physical ability is unquestioned, but in successive games against the Phillies this week I saw him make the kind of mental errors that get Little Leaguers chewed out. On Tuesday night he overran second base and got caught in a rundown. On Wednesday, he let Garry Maddox's blooper fall in front of him. God's will, I suppose.*[14]

Dickey's assessment of Clark's mental approach was not without merit. Gary Peterson wrote in *The Mercury News*:

> *If you're a Giants fan of a certain age, you remember Jack Clark fondly, a talented kid who reached the majors at 19, was an All-Star at 22 and established himself as the team's most dangerous bat in a post-Mays world.*
>
> *And you probably regard him with frustration, given he was never able to carry the Giants to the postseason, though such an act would've been akin to pulling a piano up Potrero Hill.*
>
> *And you probably allow yourself a giggle recalling the year that he inexplicably, on a couple of occasions, came jogging in from right field thinking there were three outs when there were only two. A helpful fan took to raising placards reading "One out." "Two out." "Three out, come on in."*
>
> *"I had a tendency to drift off in the outfield," he said later in his career.*[15]

As lifelong Giants fan John Maschino, who was eleven in 1978, put it:

> *The famous moment [was] Jack Clark forgetting how many outs there were in the outfield. Other players have done that.*

That's nothing new, but because Jack Clark did it . . . everybody made fun of him . . . but I think kind of in an endearing way, because that's the kind of thing Jack Clark would do . . . It made it feel like Jack Clark is like us. These ballplayers are kind of superhuman, but Jack Clark is a forgetful doofus, just like I am.[16]

But when it came to the question of motivation, Clark took exception to the implication that being born again had made him complacent. When Clark got off to an outstanding start at the plate in the spring of 1984, Filmer wrote:

"It's really tough to figure out," said Giant Manager Frank Robinson. "This guy should have always been playing like this, but for some reason he never got it together. He's always been a devoted player who's worked hard. I can't figure it out."

Some say that the problem may have been a loss of motivation. A few years ago, Clark became a born-again Christian. Baseball may have slipped a bit on his list of priorities. During those slump-ridden seasons when bad days were passed off as "God's plan to make me a better person."[17]

Since Filmer doesn't specify who the "some" are that make this allegation, it appears to be speculation. The article continued with Clark refuting the charge:

Clark dismisses any discussion about his religious beliefs having anything to do with stifling his enormous baseball talents.

"I'm having a good year and I'm still just as religious as I've ever been," he said. "None of my problems were related

to God. If it weren't for Him, I would've been a lot worse off; I may have been out of the game by now. But I kept trying because He wanted me to and now I'm realizing that my patience was worth it."[18]

Ron Fimrite, who penned a piece about Clark for *Sports Illustrated* in August 1982, wrote, "Not even his severest critics suggest that Clark doesn't give his all. His mind may wander from time to time, but many of his fielding mistakes result from overzealousness. And if he could hit in the month of April, he might yet become a Triple Crown winner."[19]

Clark may not have been able to propel the Giants to the postseason, but in two of his three seasons with the Cardinals, 1985 and 1987, the team reached the World Series.

"I don't think there's much doubt what he did for us," Herzog said in 1990, three years after Clark left the Cards. "We haven't been back to the World Series since, have we?"[20]

But if any, like Dickey, felt that becoming a Jesus follower made players passive and gave them the option to excuse every failure as "God's will," Giants fans (bred to be eternal Dodger-haters) will be pleased to hear how Clark felt about hitting his most famous home run, a three-run shot off the Dodgers' Tom Niedenfuer to clinch the National League pennant for the Cardinals in the top of the ninth inning of Game 6 of the 1985 National League Championship Series at Dodger Stadium.

In the seventh inning, with the score tied and Ozzie Smith on third base, Clark struck out against Niedenfuer. Mike Marshall hit a home run in the eighth inning to give the Dodgers a 5–4 lead.

In the top of the ninth, the Cardinals were down to their last out when Clark came up with Willie McGee on third base and Ozzie Smith on second. Instead of issuing an intentional walk, Dodger manager Tommy Lasorda decided to pitch to Clark. The former Giant smashed Niedenfuer's first pitch into the left field stands.

"It was a good pitch to hit—a fast ball, down—and I knew it was gone the minute I hit it," Clark told UPI sportswriter Aurelio Rojas.[21]

"I knew first base was open, but I thought they'd come after me because that's what they always did when I was with the Giants because they never respected us," Clark told blogger Jason Peake. "I was having a great series and I thought I could hit anything. I was on everything. And I didn't like the Dodgers. I wanted them to go down. They came after me on the first pitch and I was ready for it. It was a pretty big moment for me, my teammates, Whitey Herzog and the Cardinal fans . . . and also for the Giants' fans."[22]

As Rojas noted:

The victory washed away unhappy memories both distant and recent for Clark.

"All the way around the bases, I thought about all the bad times," said the Cardinals' first baseman, who went through a number of losing seasons with the San Francisco Giants before being traded to St. Louis in the off-season.

"As I neared home plate and saw all my teammates there, it dawned on me, 'We're going to the World Series, we're going to the World Series' . . .

"I made the big out before, and gave Marshall the opportunity to put them ahead," said Clark, a born-again Christian. "But I got a chance to redeem myself."[23]

Clark told Rick Hummel of the *St. Louis Post-Dispatch*, "There was a lot of payback for a lot of reasons. For all those years in Candlestick Park. Not only was it bad enough just having to play there, but the Dodgers kept whipping up on us every year. I had one mission. To seek and destroy everyone on that team, from Fernando Valenzuela to Orel Hershiser. I wanted it all."

Hummel wrote, "The rage in Clark almost was uncontrollable when he faced the Dodgers."

"I tried to hit it out of the stadium," Clark told him. "I didn't just want a home run. I wanted to have it be shot out of a cannon."[24]

If being born again put out Clark's competitive fire, the Dodgers would sure like an explanation.

As Hall of Famer Joe Morgan, Clark's Giants teammate in 1981 and 1982, said, "There are hitters who can get their hits in the early innings but they don't want to be up in the ninth inning with the game on the line. Jack loves to be up there in those situations. That's what he lives for."[25]

Ironically, Clark played high school baseball in Azusa, California, in the Los Angeles area, but has always been a Giants fan. Dave Anderson wrote that Clark said, with a smile, "I was a Giant fan surrounded by Dodger fans. Mays, McCovey, Cepeda, Marichal, Gaylord Perry, the Alou brothers, Jim Ray Hart, that was my team. Being drafted by the Giants was the biggest thing in my life.

"No," he added, with a pause. "finding the Lord has been the biggest thing in my life."[26]

Notes

[1] Whitey Herzog and Jonathan Pitts, *You're Missin' a Great Game: From Casey to Ozzie, the Magic of Baseball and How to Get it Back* (New York, NY: Simon & Schuster, 1999), 122.

[2] Nick Peters, "Clark Complete, Confident . . . and only 22," *The Sporting News*, August 19, 1978, 8.

[3] Nick Peters, "Clark Complete, Confident . . . and only 22," *The Sporting News*, August 19, 1978, 8.

[4] Dave Anderson, "Baseball's New Name: Jack Clark," *The New York Times*, July 11, 1978, B14.

[5] Nick Peters, "Clark Complete, Confident . . . and only 22," *The Sporting News*, August 19, 1978, 8.

[6] Albert Morch, "God and the Giants," *San Francisco Examiner*, July 31, 1978, 17.

[7] John B. Koffend, "A Born-Again Giant Hits Harder," *Us*, August 22, 1978, 26.

[8] John B. Koffend, "A Born-Again Giant Hits Harder," *Us*, August 22, 1978, 27.

[9] Joe Sargis, " 'Born-again' Jack Clark Sparks Giants Revival," *Binghamton Press and Sun-Bulletin*, July 29, 1978, 8-C.

[10] Bob Slocum, "God's Squad," *The Modesto Bee*, August 13, 1978, 51.

[11] Emery Filmer, "Clark Finally Emerges from a Giant Shadow," *Southern Connecticut Newspapers*, May 27, 1984, 55.

[12] Mike Granberry, "The Season According to Jack Clark," *Los Angeles Times*, April 10, 1980, 35.

[13] Alan Arakelian, "Clark Keeping the 'Faith' in Life," *Santa Cruz Sentinel*, July 1, 1979, 53, 56.

[14] Glenn Dickey, "What a Davis Court Victory Could Mean," *San Francisco Chronicle*, May 15, 1981, 77.

[15] Gary Peterson, "Bankruptcy Adds to the Rocky Retirement of Jack Clark," *The Mercury News*, March 23, 2018, https://www.mercurynews.com/2018/03/23/bankruptcy-adds-to-the-rocky-retirement-

of-former-giant-jack-clark first four para.

16 Lincoln A. Mitchell, *San Francisco Year Zero: Political Upheaval, Punk Rock and a Third-Place Baseball Team* (New Brunswick, NJ: Rutgers University Press, 2020), 104.

17 Emery Filmer, "Clark Finally Emerges from a Giant Shadow," *Southern Connecticut Newspapers*, May 27, 1984, 55.

18 Emery Filmer, "Clark Finally Emerges from a Giant Shadow," *Southern Connecticut Newspapers*, May 27, 1984, 55.

19 Ron Fimrite, "Jack Jumps All Over Candlestick," *Sports Illustrated*, August 23, 1982, 16.

20 Bob Nightengale, "They're Going to Go," *Los Angeles Times*, April 8, 1990, https://www.latimes.com/archives/la-xpm-1990-04-08-sp-1817-story.html para. 38.

21 Alejandro Rojas, "A Religious Man, Clark Knows the Meaning of Redemption," UPI, October 16, 1985, 1.

22 Jason Peake, "Jack the Ripper: Former Cardinals Slugger Clark Shares Stories of MLB Career at Mickey Mantle Classic," April 10, 2022, https://somo-sports.com/baseball/jack-the-ripper-former-cardinals-slugger-clark-shares-stories-of-mlb-career-at-mickey-mantle-classic para 21.

23 Alejandro Rojas, "A Religious Man, Clark Knows the Meaning of Redemption," UPI, October 16, 1985, 1.

24 Rick Hummel, "The Dodgers Didn't Walk Jack Clark in the NLCS, and the Rest is History," *St. Louis Post-Dispatch*, October 16, 2013, https://www.stltoday.com/sports/baseball/professional/the-dodgers-didnt-walk-jack-clark-in-the-nlcs-and-the-rest-is-history/article_39f77f42-7be0-5e18-b198-ba25e1912625.html para. 20-21, 26-27.

25 Glenn Dickey, *San Francisco Giants 40 Years* (San Francisco: Woodford Press, 1997), 98.

26 Dave Anderson, "Baseball's New Name: Jack Clark," *The New York Times*, July 11, 1978, B14.

Chapter 7
BOO!

Johnnie LeMaster wasn't on the Giants for his bat. The .222 lifetime hitter spent ten of his twelve major league seasons with the Giants at shortstop. The 6'2" 165-pounder played in the era when shortstops were not expected to swing a big bat. Players like Mark Belanger, Don Kessinger, Dal Maxvill, Gene Michael, and Bud Harrelson were small in stature, did not hit for power, but earned their keep with excellent glovework.

LeMaster hit an inside-the-park home run at Candlestick Park in his first major league at-bat in September 1975. He would only hit twenty-one more round-trippers in his career.

LeMaster's first season in which he played in over one hundred games was 1978. Dave Newhouse of the *Oakland Tribune* wrote, "In 1978, he became a reborn Christian and a member of the 'God Squad,' a group of strongly religious Giants who incurred the fans' wrath. Those Giants teams were perceived as too goody-goody, yet San Francisco nearly won the division title in 1982."[1]

Newhouse didn't mention that they also challenged for the division crown in 1978. But that's when the boos began for LeMaster—specifically, according to writer Sam Miller, on April 18.

He noted, "The Giants had ace John Montefusco on the mound, and he pitched beautifully, but his teammates managed only a single hit. LeMaster made a throwing error that led to a run, and the Giants lost 1–0. The fans booed the goat, LeMaster. And they just . . . never stopped. They developed a habit and never bothered to break it."²

On April 26, Glenn Schwarz of the Examiner reported:

The first chorus of boos drifted out from the Candlestick stands and reached Johnnie LeMaster's ears a week ago. By the weekend, you didn't need a scorecard to know who was coming to bat for the San Francisco Giants. As the catcalls increased, LeMaster bit his lower lip and told himself to ignore the noise.

"It's something I have to live with. The fans pay their money and can boo when they want," the Giants shortstop said. "You just can't let it get to you." . . .

It was no coincidence that it began after LeMaster made a throwing error behind John Montefusco, leading to an unearned run for Atlanta and a 1–0 defeat for the Count.

*"I would say the error had a little to do with the boos. Maybe a lot," LeMaster said, "But I haven't hit yet either."*³

In late May, Jim Kaplan of *Sports Illustrated* wrote, "Another contribution has been the defensive work of shortstop Johnnie LeMaster. A woeful hitter with a weak swing and a .202 average, he has saved one-run wins against the Pirates and Cardinals with backhand stabs in the ninth inning."⁴

After the Giants went 6–1 in a week in mid-June, Herman Weiskopf wrote in *Sports Illustrated*, "San Francisco fans, who earlier had booed Johnnie LeMaster for his lackluster hitting, cheered his slick fielding at shortstop."⁵

But, as Miller said, the booing resumed. And when the Giants returned to their losing ways in 1979 (71–91 record), the fans, for some reason, directed their displeasure at LeMaster.

As Miller put it, "It would be too emotionally draining, too real, for Giants fans to hate all 25 players on their losing club, so they invented a myth that LeMaster alone was the scapegoat."[6]

"The only thing I could figure out is I would make an error at the wrong time of the game, or maybe not get a base hit at the right time of the game," LeMaster said. "Our record wasn't the greatest the whole time that I played there. Maybe they needed somebody to let their frustration out on, or their anger."[7]

His wife, Debbie, kiddingly suggested he change his name to Boo. LeMaster ran with the idea and asked equipment manager Eddie Logan to make a jersey with "BOO" on the back in place of his last name. After a couple of weeks, on July 23, 1979, at Candlestick, LeMaster got up the courage to wear it in a game. The only teammate who knew LeMaster was going to pull the stunt was Rob Andrews.

Manager Altobelli, who didn't have the best eyesight, asked Andrews why LeMaster had "Bob" on the back of his jersey. That broke up everybody in the dugout. The caper was short-lived. LeMaster only got to wear the jersey in the field in the top half of the first inning before General Manager Spec Richardson intervened, fired the equipment manager, and ordered LeMaster to put on his regular jersey.[1]

---

[1] Although LeMaster remembers wearing the "Boo" jersey for only half an inning, another account says he wore it for a couple of innings and had one at bat with the jersey on, in which he popped out to third: https://pebblehunting.substack.com/p/they-boo-shortstops-dont-they. There is an Associated Press photo of him batting with the jersey on here (the caption says the game was on July 24, which is incorrect; he wore the Boo jersey on July 23, 1979): https://www.sfchronicle.com/sports/article/Where-are-they-now-Catching-up-with-former-14465433.php#photo-18171002.

"But, when the game was over," LeMaster related, "where do you think every single newspaper reporter, every TV camera in the whole San Francisco Bay Area was at? And I mean I had mikes in front of my face like you wouldn't believe. But here's the thing about it. The fans loved it. The reporters loved it. They ate it up. My general manager fined me $500 for being out of uniform. But it was the best fine that I'd ever had. Eddie Logan got his job back and all ended up well."[8]

LeMaster had no regrets. Years later, he told the high school baseball players he coached, "Every once in a while, it's not bad to do something a little bit crazy. Sometimes doing something a little bit crazy makes people realize you're as human as they are."[9]

But when the novelty of the "Boo" jersey prank wore off, fans went back to booing him. Newhouse wrote, "Nobody who has played for the Oakland A's and San Francisco Giants—and LeMaster played for both—had to endure the loud, intense, sustained booing Johnnie Boo suffered through as a Giants shortstop."[10]

"I was getting booed pretty bad," recalled the shortstop. "Vile things were said."[11]

Even when the worm began to turn, LeMaster could not catch a break. As Art Rosenbaum wrote in the *Chronicle* in June 1981:

> *For LeMaster, this was beginning to be an enjoyable season. He had been booed when introduced for the season opener at Candlestick Park—before the first ball was gloved around here. Since then, through the early weeks, it was LeMaster's steady fielding that brought praise from his pitchers and the fans. Too many errors were being committed but at other positions. So now Johnnie is in a new role—hero.*[12]

So what happened? The major league players called for a strike, which lasted from June 12 to August 9, wiping out 38 percent of the schedule.

LeMaster admitted the booing affected him but said he has never been bitter about it.

Giants broadcaster Duane Kuiper, a second baseman who formed a double-play combination with LeMaster for three years, said:

> *When you're playing before 6,000 on a Tuesday night at Candlestick Park, you can hear what they say, and they know you can hear. It's hard to have fun in those conditions. Once the fans determine a whipping boy, they can make it rough on you. I think Johnnie was very sensitive. But we clearly played on the worst infield in baseball. We were never allowed to use that as an excuse, but the wind would tear up the infield and it would dry out.*[13]

"Sometimes you had to reach down real deep to not let it bother you," said LeMaster of the booing. "You want to please your manager, you want to please your teammates, but when it's all said and done, it's about trying to please your fans to the best of your ability."[14]

The devout Christian added, "It would be hard for anybody to get through it if they didn't realize what Jesus Christ went through. When he was on the cross, the mob was yelling, 'Crucify him, crucify him.' You realize if he could go through something like that, you can go through anything. That's what got me through it."[15]

In August 1979 LeMaster talked with the *Los Angeles Times* about his spiritual journey: "I think the biggest thing that has happened to me is I have inner peace. All my troubles, I just said, 'Hey, Lord, these are yours. You take care of 'em. I'm going to forget about 'em.' It just frees you to go out and live your life the way the Man wants you to and have no worries."[16]

At the Giants last game at Candlestick in 1999 (the Giants moved to their new stadium in 2000), LeMaster and other former players gathered for the occasion. Right on cue, the fans booed him.

"It was kind of a joke," said LeMaster. "They've had two Johnnie LeMaster Nights since I retired. It's unbelievable how the fans come up to me and say, 'We don't think you were treated right while you were here.' "[17]

He ended his career with a twenty-game stint with the Oakland A's in 1987. Teammate Reggie Jackson questioned him about the fans booing him on a regular basis in San Francisco. Jackson told him, "People don't boo nobodies. You're somebody." LeMaster said the comment "made me feel like a million dollars."[18]

He said, "I still have that 'Boo' jersey and collectors from New York call me all the time wanting to buy it, but I can't part with it."[19]

As Lincoln Mitchell wrote in his book, *San Francisco Year Zero*, which focused on events in the city in 1978, including the Giants' run for the pennant:

> During his time with the Giants, LeMaster was a somewhat polarizing figure for Giants fans. Many booed him aggressively and could only see his faults as a player. Others felt he was treated unfairly by the fans and was a fine fielder whose anemic bat would have been less conspicuous on a better offensive team. One of the latter is Charles A. Fracchia Jr., the son of the prominent San Francisco historian,

who was thirteen years old during that 1978 season and still occasionally wears a replica Johnnie LeMaster "Boo" jersey when he watches the Giants now. Of LeMaster, Fracchia told me, "I like him. I felt he was kind of a glue on the infield."[20]

Notes

[1] Dave Newhouse, "Reviled LeMaster Finds Peace Coaching in Appalachian Home," *Oakland Tribune*, August 6, 2002, 1.

[2] Sam Miller, "They Boo Shortstops, Don't They?" May 10, 2023, https://pebblehunting.substack.com/p/they-boo-shortstops-dont-they para 16.

[3] Glenn Schwarz, "LeMaster Still Battles the Boos," *San Francisco Examiner*, June 6, 1980, 43.

[4] Larry Keith, "These Giants are Jolly Blue," *San Francisco Examiner*, June 6, 1980, 22.

[5] Herman Weiskopf, "The Week (June 11-17)," *Sports Illustrated*, June 26, 1978, 53.

[6] Sam Miller, "They Boo Shortstops, Don't They?" May 10, 2023, https://pebblehunting.substack.com/p/they-boo-shortstops-dont-they para 17.

[7] Tom Fitzgerald, "Where are they now? Catching up with former Giants shortstop Johnnie LeMaster," *San Francisco Chronicle*, September 25, 2019, https://www.sfchronicle.com/sports/article/Where-are-they-now-Catching-up-with-former-14465433.php para. 14.

[8] Johnnie LeMaster, "Short Stop with a Shortstop," podcast, episode 1, "The Boo Jersey," https://www.facebook.com/watch/?v=473876187141561

[9] Tom Fitzgerald, "Where are they now? Catching up with former Giants shortstop Johnnie LeMaster," *San Francisco Chronicle*, September 25, 2019, https://www.sfchronicle.com/sports/article/Where-are-they-now-Catching-up-with-former-14465433.php para 19.

[10] Dave Newhouse, "Reviled LeMaster Finds Peace Coaching in Ap-

palachian Home," *Oakland Tribune*, August 6, 2002, 1.

[11] Dave Newhouse, "Reviled LeMaster Finds Peace Coaching in Appalachian Home," *Oakland Tribune*, August 6, 2002, 1.

[12] Art Rosenbaum, "LeMaster Thinks About the Future," *San Francisco Chronicle*, June 26, 1981, 59.

[13] Dave Newhouse, "Reviled LeMaster Finds Peace Coaching in Appalachian Home," *Oakland Tribune*, August 6, 2002, 1.

[14] Tom Fitzgerald, "Where are they now? Catching up with former Giants shortstop Johnnie LeMaster," *San Francisco Chronicle*, September 25, 2019, https://www.sfchronicle.com/sports/article/Where-are-they-now-Catching-up-with-former-14465433.php para. 27.

[15] Tom Fitzgerald, "Where are they now? Catching up with former Giants shortstop Johnnie LeMaster," *San Francisco Chronicle*, September 25, 2019, https://www.sfchronicle.com/sports/article/Where-are-they-now-Catching-up-with-former-14465433.php para 28.

[16] William Endicott, " 'Born Again' Ballplayers on Increase," *Los Angeles Times*, August 31, 1979, 28.

[17] Tom Fitzgerald, "Where are they now? Catching up with former Giants shortstop Johnnie LeMaster," *San Francisco Chronicle*, September 25, 2019, https://www.sfchronicle.com/sports/article/Where-are-they-now-Catching-up-with-former-14465433.php para. 6.

[18] Tom Fitzgerald, "Where are they now? Catching up with former Giants shortstop Johnnie LeMaster," *San Francisco Chronicle*, September 25, 2019, https://www.sfchronicle.com/sports/article/Where-are-they-now-Catching-up-with-former-14465433.php para. 26.

[19] Ed Attanasio, "The TGG Interview: Johnnie LeMaster," https://thisgreatgame.com/johnnie-lemaster para. 7.

[20] Lincoln A. Mitchell, *San Francisco Year Zero: Political Upheaval, Punk Rock and a Third-Place Baseball Team* (New Brunswick, NJ: Rutgers University Press, 2020), 55.

Chapter 8
Mike Ivie

Ivie had a turbulent time adjusting psychologically to the demands of professional baseball. But he kept at it in an eleven-year career interrupted from time to time by meltdowns for which he sought help in understanding.

At 6'4" and 210 pounds, Ivie was an All-State fullback and linebacker in high school. Colleges would have offered him football scholarships, but he wanted to play baseball.

The San Diego Padres selected Ivie first overall in the 1970 Major League Baseball draft as a catcher. That created high expectations which overwhelmed the seventeen-year-old.

"You're supposed to be the best out of all the high school and semipro players in the country," Ivie said. "When I started out I was lost."[1]

He told *The New York Times*, "I was an only child, and everybody expected me to be the best player in the world. My dad wanted me to be the best in the Little League . . . The pressure started building up."[2]

In the minor leagues, he developed a case of the yips—he couldn't throw the ball back to the pitcher.

A source close to the Padres told the *Chronicle's* Bruce Jenkins:

It goes all the way back to the day we signed Ivie in 1970. He was the nation's No. 1 draft choice, an outstanding high school catcher from Georgia. We flew him out to the park that day and had him work out with the club before the game.

There was a screen in front of the mound, and Mike kept hitting it with his throws. One of our coaches, Chris Canizzaro, was kidding him. "That's why they're sending you to Walla Walla, kid," and that bothered Mike. He developed a phobia about throwing the ball back to the pitcher.

The next spring down in Yuma, he got into the habit of double-pumping before his throws. Preston Gomez, who was managing the club then, got on him about it and Mike couldn't take it. When the workout was over he said he wasn't going to catch any more and flew back home to Georgia. He was there almost two months before he reported to the minors.[3]

When Don Zimmer was the Padres manager in 1973, Ivie tried catching again.

"He was just super," said Zimmer. "I thought we were set for ten years. But one day he called me into his room and was crying. 'I just don't want to catch anymore,' he said. And that was that."[4]

"If Mike had played out his career behind the plate," said Bob Fontaine, former general manager of the Padres, "he would've become a candidate for the Hall of Fame. He had the softest, quickest hands you ever saw, a strong, accurate arm, plus all that size and power."[5]

Ivie went AWOL again when he thought the Padres had not kept a promise to bring him up to the majors. Once in the big leagues with San Diego, he continued to have issues. Manager John McNamara suspended him for two games in May 1977 because he refused to play third base after practicing all spring at first.

He ended up playing most of the season at first base and batted .272. In the winter of 1978, the Padres traded him to the Giants.

"I feel like a kid at Christmas," Ivie told the Associated Press during spring training. "I can't wait to get to the ballpark every morning. It's a new start for me, and I couldn't be happier about it."[6]

Ivie went on to discuss his time with the Padres:

"I consider those years kind of a test," said Ivie, who has become a born-again Christian. "Now God is giving me a chance to begin again. He blessed me with a lot of physical talent, but I wasn't grown up enough to handle things. I've grown up a lot in the past few years, have become a parent, for one thing, and my faith has made me able to understand things better now than I did in the past.

"Now what I've got to do," Ivie continued, "is what I know I can do, fulfill my promise. I always knew I could play the game, could be good at it, but other things kept getting in my way. I feel really lucky; I've got a lot of experience, I'm still just 25 years old, and I'm getting a brand new start."[7]

All that promise came together in 1978, when Ivie hit .308 and belted those two pinch-hit grand-slam home runs, a record shared with four other major leaguers.

In late May 1978, an injury to starting catcher Hill meant the Giants had only one catcher, Mike Sadek. The *Chronicle* noted:

Mike Ivie, who has had trouble breaking into the starting lineup despite his .391 average, was a highly-regarded catcher in high school and could seemingly step right in but he won't do it.

"I'm through with catching," he said last night. "I wouldn't even do it as a last resort. That's the most dangerous position in baseball, and I'm not going to get myself hurt. It also takes away from your concentration on hitting. I'd rather wait for opportunities when they come at first base or the outfield."

Ivie temporarily quit baseball in 1972, having refused to catch for the San Diego Padres, and the bitter memories remain. "I don't even want to rehash it," he said. "I'm a new man now."[8]

He had an even better year in 1979, smashing twenty-seven home runs and driving in eighty-nine runs to go along with a .286 batting average. But trials awaited him that would cause emotional turmoil that even his faith was not able to subdue.

While cleaning a hunting knife in the off-season, Ivie cut the flexor tendon in the little finger of his right hand. He could not bend the finger. In January 1980 in order to stretch the tendon into correct position, surgery was performed down the right side of Ivie's palm, almost to the heel of his hand.

His finger was in a cast for six weeks. A portion of Ivie's upper arm was tied to the tip of his finger so that the finger would remain bent, and his right wrist was frozen in a bent-forward position. When the cast came off, Ivie had lost much of the strength in his right arm. He also injured his left ankle on opening day. The injuries created a lot of mental stress.

"My talent is my hitting," he said, "and I couldn't do it.

Maybe I think differently than other people, but when you've had a body that's been like a bull, you expect it to perform. I went to spring training and saw guys who didn't have nearly my ability hitting the ball twice as far as I could. I wondered if I was ever going to get better."[9]

"The doctors said he was coming along great," said his wife, Pam, "but in his mind he wasn't doing as well as he could. That's when he began to get depressed. People can understand when you say you have cancer, but how many understand when you say you have mental depression?"[10]

The problem was not just in Ivie's mind. The pinkie finger is responsible for 50 percent of a person's hand strength.[11]

On June 5, 1980, the Giants placed Ivie on the fifteen-day disabled list for "mental exhaustion."

"The frustration built up in him. He was visibly upset, with not hitting, his hand hurting, his ankle hurting," manager Dave Bristol said. "A combination of things just ate away at him. It wasn't a family problem. It's baseball related."[12]

Giants' pitcher Tom Griffin, who was also a teammate of Ivie's in San Diego, said, "He's an extremely sensitive person, always has been. I don't know about that reputation as a malingerer. I can see where guys might think that . . . I don't think he is. It's just that it bothers him tremendously when he can't perform. It really eats away at him."[13]

Ivie returned from the disabled list, but on June 25 he stunned the Giants by announcing he was retiring from baseball. He was just twenty-seven years old.

"Peace of mind is what I want," he told the *Examiner*. "I just want to live like a normal person. I want to have a simple life: a little place, a seven-to-five job, Saturdays and

Sundays off, vacations and picnics with the family. I want to be a husband to my wife, a father to my two kids."[14]

He told the *Chronicle*, "I've been going through a lot of stress and strain with my hand not recuperating the way it should. It's a really, really hard time for me trying to cope with the injury and rehabilitation."[15]

A few of his teammates had a talk with him.

"Gary Lavelle, Bob Knepper and Johnnie LeMaster all were helpful to me," said Ivie. "They are all good Christians like I am. The day I decided to retire, they sat down with me until 1 o'clock in the morning, right there in that hotel room, trying to get me to change my mind. But I wasn't listening to what they were saying. My mind was too full of anxiety to really understand what they were trying to say."[16]

Glenn Schwarz of the *Examiner* wrote, "The clubhouse consensus seemed to be that he was sincere, but that he will have second thoughts about tossing away the seven-figure contract that took effect this year. 'I'm hoping this doesn't last all year,' said one of Ivie's friends, shortstop Johnnie LeMaster. 'I don't really think he wants to quit.'"[17]

LeMaster was right. Ivie, who said he was on the verge of a nervous breakdown when he retired, consulted with a psychiatrist and also got an encouraging call from Willie McCovey, his teammate on the Padres and the Giants. The call convinced him to ask the Giants to reinstate him, and they did in July.

Upon his return, he told Terence Moore of the *Examiner*, "I retired when I did because of nagging physical injuries, general stress and anxiety overall. But that's in the past. Since then, I've talked to counselors, close friends and teammates about what I should do. They all have helped me a great deal. I couldn't have done it without them or the Lord or Mr. [Bob] Lurie or [General Manager] Spec Richardson."[18]

Ivie had a spiritual reset, which Moore discussed:

> *The first baseman left the club last month with "mental exhaustion." But he has returned to the Giants with an ever-present smile that rivals that of Lavelle.*
>
> *"He'll put you through trials and tribulations and He'll use every resource to help you find happiness in your heart," said Ivie in his best Georgian twang. "It would have been twice as hard for me to come back if I hadn't have believed in the Lord...*
>
> *"I used to read that King James version of the Bible—you know, the one with all those 'thou arts' and 'thou fors,'" he said, shaking his head. "Heck, I couldn't understand it. Then I went out and got me one of them living Bibles. And I've been reading Proverbs and that's really helped out.*
>
> *"But you know, things have changed around here. It used to be that if you were a Christian that you had to sneak a Bible into your locker and read it there. That ain't the case anymore."*[19]

In a July 1978 interview, Ivie traced his born-again experience to early 1976 when he was a San Diego Padre. Prior to that, he said, he was a "fence-riding Christian. I wanted Him when I needed Him, and when I was doing good, I let Him go by the wayside. I'm with Him now through thick and thin."[20]

He said he committed his life to Jesus after watching how the born-again Christians on the Padres handled adversity, noting that they "always seemed to have a smile and a bubbly feeling, even when things were going wrong."[21]

It would be nice if being born again solved all of one's

emotional problems, but that, as Ivie found out, is not the case.

When Frank Robinson was hired to manage the Giants in 1981, he went the extra mile with Ivie.

Robinson told the *New York Daily News* a week before the season began:

> *I've spoken to him. I had a speaking engagement in Atlanta [Ivie's home during the offseason] and I had a chance to talk to him for quite a while. I could have done it by phone, but I'd rather do it face to face. I wanted him to have an opportunity to know me better and what I expect of him. It was a very good talk. I went away with the feeling that he is ready to concentrate on baseball and go all out.*[22]

Robinson elaborated to *The Boston Globe* about that visit:

> *I was pleasantly impressed. It's my impression that he's just a young country boy who was in the majors as a teenager and overwhelmed by the whole thing. He's a player with a lot of talent, but he's a kid without much self-confidence. He had been close to [Dave] Bristol when Bristol was a coach, but when Dave became manager and took the no-nonsense hard line, it apparently devastated Ivie. I don't pretend to say that I've got new ideas, but Ivie's apparently a kid who needs a pat on the back. I'm not ashamed to do that. Kissing someone's behind is one thing, but a manager has to pat some guys back there.*[23]

One reporter claimed that Ivie retiring and unretiring caused division on the Giants. Joe Stein wrote, "While some Giants openly resent Ivie, who walked out on the team last season, others such as Johnnie LeMaster and Gary Lavelle have been quick to offer aid and comfort. The situation has strained club morale . . . "[24]

If some of the Giants did "openly resent" Ivie, it is curious that Stein did not get a quote from any of them. Ironically, the day Stein's article was published, the Giants traded Ivie to the Houston Astros.

When Robinson tabbed Enos Cabell to start the season at first base instead of Ivie, Ivie demanded a trade. On April 20, he got his wish. But after playing fourteen games with his new team, the Astros, he was found weeping in the locker room after a poor performance.

"I thought coming here [to Houston] was a chance to go back to square one," Ivie said. "But I didn't know anybody. I'd been to spring training with the Giants. Then I found myself pressing again . . . I had lost my confidence."[25]

The Astros put him on the disabled list, where he remained through the fifty-day strike that season. He joined the team in San Francisco on August 10 when the strike ended. There he read a newspaper detailing his emotional problems and flew back to Houston.

"He stayed about two minutes," said Astros manager Bill Virdon. "He was probably nervous about going back to the West Coast, anyway. Then he got upset and left without telling anybody."[26]

Art Spander wrote about it:

> *This was to be a major test for Mike Ivie. Now a member of the Houston Astros, he was going to return to the two cities where he previously played, San Francisco and San Diego, was going to see old friends, confront his demons. He was so confident. Then he ran away.*
>
> *It had gone so well. He was out of the hospital after once*

more suffering "mental exhaustion," had taken hold of his fears, was practicing with the team. He would not be placed on the active roster for a while, but this road trip, this post-strike beginning, would prove he had conquered the apprehension that set him down like no opposing pitcher ever could.

And then? "Then he got up at the hotel Monday morning," said Dave Roberts, Ivie's roommate, "and said he wasn't ready. He didn't want to go out and fail again. He got permission and flew home."[27]

Roberts noted, "He's made progress. He was coming along just fine. But it's still going to take time."[28]

Virdon added, "He's the only person who really knows what's wrong. He's the only one who will know when he's ready. What he's going through must be very tough. I feel sorry for him."[29]

According to Ivie's Astros teammate, pitcher Don Sutton, the Astros organization as a whole was very understanding. Sutton, himself a born-again Christian, said:

This is a unique club. If you came here with a divorce situation, a death in the family, an illness or mental exhaustion or whatever, our club would be one which is genuinely interested in you. It's something I've really enjoyed about being here. I haven't seen anyone ostracized or criticized for it. They've been helpful and supportive. This is probably the best collection of good friends I have ever played with on a baseball team.[30]

The Astros reactivated Ivie in September 1981. But early in 1982, he asked for and was given his release. He signed with the Detroit Tigers, where he had a bit of a renaissance that year, hitting fourteen home runs in only 259 at-bats.

As Ivie told writer Dan Holmes of vintagedetroit.com, "Hey, a fish doesn't forget how to swim."[31]

But the Tigers released him in May 1983 and he never returned to professional baseball.

After reading the March 2014 article by Holmes, Ivie's son Steve posted this comment in May of that year: "Thanks for the clear explanation of Mike's career. He is my father, and I have heard these stories from him a million times. I completely understand the pressures an athlete has to deal with playing in bigs. Mike is doing great now!!"[32]

The pressure was off.

Notes

[1] Bruce Newman, "He has Georgia on His Mind," *Sports Illustrated*, July 29, 1980, 36.

[2] Joseph Durso, "Ivie: A Player Who Was Afraid to Fail," *The New York Times*, September 3, 1981, D-25.

[3] Bruce Jenkins, "Why Ivie is Depressed," *San Francisco Chronicle*, June 7, 1980, 44.

[4] Bruce Jenkins, "Why Ivie is Depressed," *San Francisco Chronicle*, June 7, 1980, 44.

[5] Bruce Newman, "He has Georgia on His Mind," *Sports Illustrated*, July 29, 1980, 36.

[6] Associated Press, "Mike Ivie Happy to Get New Start with Giants," *Eureka Times Standard*, April 1, 1978, 9.

[7] Associated Press, "Mike Ivie Happy to Get New Start with Giants," *Eureka Times Standard*, April 1, 1978, 9.

[8] Bruce Jenkins, "Knepper Beats Astros, 1-0, on Five-Hitter," *San Francisco Chronicle*, May 31, 1978, 52.

[9] Bruce Newman, "He has Georgia on His Mind," *Sports Illustrated*,

July 29, 1980, 37.

[10] Bruce Newman, "He has Georgia on His Mind," *Sports Illustrated*, July 29, 1980, 37.

[11] Dana Scarton, "Gel Along Without a Pinkie? It's Tougher Than You Might Think," *The New York Times*, December 15, 2008, D-5.

[12] Glenn Schwarz, "Mike Ivie Mystery Deepens," *San Francisco Examiner*, June 6, 1980, 57.

[13] Bruce Jenkins, "Why Ivie is Depressed," *San Francisco Chronicle*, June 7, 1980, 44.

[14] Glenn Schwarz, "Ivie Retires, and Giants Ask—Why?" *San Francisco Examiner*, June 26, 1980, 67.

[15] Ira Miller, "Now Ivie Says He May Play Again," *San Francisco Chronicle*, June 28, 1980, 41.

[16] Terence Moore, "Mike Ivie Tells His Story," *San Francisco Examiner*, July 15, 1980, 52.

[17] Glenn Schwarz, "Ivie Retires, and Giants Ask—Why?" *San Francisco Examiner*, June 26, 1980, 68.

[18] Terence Moore, "Mike Ivie Tells His Story," *San Francisco Examiner*, July 15, 1980, 51.

[19] Terence Moore, "The Giants' Bible Brigade," *San Francisco Examiner*, July 27, 1980, 31.

[20] Albert Morch, "God and the Giants," *San Francisco Examiner*, July 31, 1978, 21.

[21] Albert Morch, "God and the Giants," *San Francisco Examiner*, July 31, 1978, 21.

[22] Norm Miller, "Robby Won't Be as Stern with Giants," *New York Daily News*, April 3, 1981, 258.

[23] Peter Gammons, "Frank's Back," *The Boston Globe*, February 17, 1981, 29–30.

[24] Joe Stein, "Frisco Has Giant Factions," *Caldwell-Burleson* (Texas) *Star*, April 20, 1981, 5.

[25] Joseph Durso, "Ivie: A Player Who Was Afraid to Fail," *The New York Times*, September 3, 1981, D-21.

[26] Joseph Durso, "Ivie: A Player Who Was Afraid to Fail," *The New York Times*, September 3, 1981, D-21.

[27] Art Spander, "Ivie's Sad Battle with Reality," *San Francisco Examiner*, August 12, 1981, 63.

[28] Art Spander, "Ivie's Sad Battle with Reality," *San Francisco Examiner*, August 12, 1981, 63.

[29] Art Spander, "Ivie's Sad Battle with Reality," *San Francisco Examiner*, August 12, 1981, 63.

[30] Charles Bricker, "Sutton, Astros Tolerant of Ivie's Behavior," *San Jose Mercury*, August 13, 1981, 89.

[31] Dan Holmes, "Number One Pick Mike Ivie Battled Emotional Troubles in Career that Ended with the Tigers," VintageDetroit.com, March 9, 2014, https://www.vintagedetroit.com/mike-ivie-battled-emotional-troubles-in-career-that-ended-with-detroit-tigers para 17.

[32] Dan Holmes, "Number One Pick Mike Ivie Battled Emotional Troubles in Career that Ended with the Tigers," VintageDetroit.com, March 9, 2014, https://www.vintagedetroit.com/mike-ivie-battled-emotional-troubles-in-career-that-ended-with-detroit-tigers comments.

Chapter 9
The Other Guys

After asking Jesus to come into his life during winter ball in 1975, Gary Lavelle returned to the Giants for the 1976 season and, whenever the opportunity presented itself, began to share his faith with his teammates.

"Because I have a personal relationship with Jesus," said Lavelle, "I feel compelled to share it. Jesus blesses us. He's with us in our good and bad moments."[1]

As author Duane Sandul noted, "Some have responded quickly to Lavelle's invitation to know Jesus; some have ignored it; and some, including his roommate, Marc Hill, have been exposed to the gospel and the Christian life style for several years before making a personal commitment."[2]

Among those whom Lavelle influenced toward a born-again experience were Bob Knepper, Rob Andrews, Jack Clark, Marc Hill, and Randy Moffitt.

As Sandul wrote, "The number of Christians grew so quickly on the Giants team in 1978 and 1979 that insiders facetiously waited to see who would be next to be baptized by Lavelle in a swimming pool."[3]

There were some Giants during the God Squad era who were Christians but, for whatever reason, did not receive much media attention for their faith. They included Hill, Terry Whitfield, four-time National League batting champion Bill Madlock, outfielder Larry Herndon, and pitchers Moffitt, Tom Griffin, and Dave Roberts.

Glenn Schwarz wrote in the *Examiner* in June 1979, "The

Giants ever-growing born-again Christian clique has expanded by at least three people this year. Dave Roberts and Tom Griffin brought their beliefs with them from other clubs. Marc Hill now says, 'I gave my life to the Lord this spring.' Hill's road roommate has been Baseball Chapel leader Gary Lavelle."[4]

Writing in October 1979 about the spread of born-again Christianity in major league baseball, William Endicott of the *Los Angeles Times* noted, "The movement has drawn particular attention in San Francisco because the Giants, while finishing fourth in the National League's western division, lead the league in what has come to be known locally as 'God Squadders.' They have 12 members including a coach, Tom Haller, and at least two potential superstars, Jack Clark and first baseman Mike Ivie."[5]

Whitfield, a left-handed hitting outfielder, was a key cog in the Giants' offense in 1978. A line drive hitter, Whitfield was remarkably consistent at the plate in his four seasons with the club, hitting .285 in 1977, .289 in 1978, .287 in 1979, and .296 in 1980.

One of the quieter members of the team, Whitfield didn't create controversy that resulted in headlines as did some of his more outspoken God Squad teammates. But he did discuss his faith with the press.

In 1977, *The* (Roseville, California) *Press-Tribune* wrote:

> *Terry is one of the bachelors on the Giants ball club and he's settled into an apartment on Twin Peaks in San Francisco. But you won't find him making the singles scene on Union Street. He prefers keeping a more modest profile instead of the playboy image. That modesty may stem from Terry's upbringing and the influence exerted upon him by cousins*

and uncles who were reverends and pastors in the Southern California area. As you talk with Terry terms like "God-fearing," "With God's will" and "Thank God" all creep into the conversation with regularity. Terry is a regular at the Giants' chapel services on Sunday mornings.[6]

The *San Francisco Examiner* shared this in July 1978:

Outfielder Terry Whitfield's religious roots run deep. The 25-year-old long-ball hitter's uncle and grandfather are preachers in Arizona. "When I was a kid and we played house, I always wanted to play the part of the preacher. My father taught me to do the best I can. God gave me the ability to play ball a little better than the other guy, so it's up to me to go out there and play my heart out."

. . . Whitfield, since he arrived in San Francisco from the Yankees last year, has noticed the growth in attendance at the team's Sunday chapel services. "It's not an organized campaign, but it is growing on its own."[7]

Madlock's Chicago Cubs teammate Don Kessinger led him to a relationship with Jesus in 1974.

"I was one of those guys who thought I was a Christian because I went to church while I was growing up," said Madlock, a Giant from 1977 to 1979. "As an athlete I had money, but there was something missing."[8]

He told the *Examiner* in July 1978, "I grew up a Baptist in Decatur, Ill., but my real awakening came when I got to the majors. Suddenly, I had all those material thank-yous, you know, like money, and I could buy whatever I wanted. Success comes so quickly. It was like a dream come true. Then I realized I still had an empty feeling inside, so I began searching."[9]

In 1978 Madlock displayed a sign in large, colorful letters above his clubhouse locker that read, "Only Jesus Fills Voids."[10]

Right-handed relief specialist Randy Moffitt, a Giant from 1972 to 1981, is the brother of tennis great Billie Jean King.

"At the age of 22, I felt that something was missing," said Moffitt. "I started talking with Lavelle and I saw how his faith had changed him. Everything seemed to be in order in his life."[11]

He had a spiritual rebirth in 1978, and Lavelle baptized him and his wife, Pamela, in a pool in Arizona.

Dave Roberts was a Giant for just part of the 1979 season. He had been born again in 1972 while a Houston Astro.

"He literally turned my life around," Roberts said of Jesus. "He made my marriage better. He improved my family life with the kids. He gave me happiness that material things never did—or could. I learned that only Jesus can provide happiness."[12]

Roberts and Tom Griffin were teammates with the Astros from 1972 to 1975. After Roberts became a believer, he shared his newfound faith with Griffin, who said:

> *I didn't really understand what he was talking about. If someone had asked me if I was a Christian, I would have said, "Yes, I go to church on Christmas and Easter and sometimes in between. I'm a pretty good guy, and I was born in America." I thought those features made one a Christian . . . I knew there was a God and I knew there was a Christ, but I didn't know you could have any kind of a relationship until I started to talk with Dave.*[13]

When Griffin understood, he gave his life to Jesus in spring 1973. Traded from Houston to San Diego and then to the California Angels, Griffin found himself without a job at age thirty when the Angels released him in 1978.

"I didn't know what I was going to do," said Griffin. "At that particular point I reasoned with myself that if I professed to be a Christian and if I had faith, then I was just going to have to put my trust and faith in the Lord to an all-out test. So I prayed, 'Lord, I want to play baseball.' I left it with Him."[14]

The only team that invited him to spring training in 1979 was the Giants, which surprised Griffin because San Francisco was already rich in pitchers. He had the second-best spring training of all the Giants pitchers and made the club as a short-inning reliever. When Griffin made the final cut, Glenn Schwarz of the *Examiner* wrote:

> *"I feel very thankful to the good Lord," said Griffin, an addition to the club's already-large contingent of born-again Christians. "I obviously wondered if I could make this club, but I worked hard and I've never felt quite so comfortable as I have this spring. (Pitching coach) Larry Shepard didn't have to pay a whole lot of attention to me—there are a whole lot of stars here—but he did. I appreciated that."*[15]

Griffin remained a Giant through the 1981 season.

Was the born-again presence causing a problem in the clubhouse? In his July 1978 *Examiner* article, "God and the Giants," Albert Morch wrote:

> *By all reports, those who have not joined the religious ranks have been extremely tolerant. Absent are the nickname*

> *labels, such as "Jesus freak," that a non-joiner might be tempted to use. "I guess it's because they're not trying to turn it into one big revival meeting," said one uncommitted player, "They respect us. We respect them."* [16]

Mike Ivie told Morch, "There is no other team like the Giants in the majors. We love each other, and are able to give each other a lift when we're feeling down. We don't actively seek converts... we let them see it through our actions, and the inner peace we've achieved. It's like being on a stage. We falter sometimes but if we were perfect, we wouldn't be here on earth."[17]

Bob Slocum of the *Modesto (California) Bee* wrote, "Willie McCovey, a non-religious Giant, but a team leader and spokesman, looks at it this way: 'The players on this club are very tolerant towards one another. But I think the religious element of this club is blown out of proportion. Every club has it. This one is just a little more vocal about it. There are no fanatics here. It's a good atmosphere.' "[18]

Not that the born-again Giants escaped some good-natured ribbing from their teammates. As John B. Koffend wrote in *Us* magazine, "At least seven Giant players and one coach profess to be born-again Christians. Naturally enough, they take a fair amount of joshing from the unanointed members of the club. The 'beautiful brothers,' as they are sometimes called, cannot quaff a beer or ogle a bikini without being reminded that the true believer is above such things."[19]

But the overall impact of so many born-again players on one team seemed to be positive. Morch concluded:

Whatever's happened is readily apparent to the Giants' faithful. Examiner photographer Bill Nichols, a veteran of more than 25 years covering professional sporting events, said, "It's unreal. I can't explain it, but I feel it." It's also obvious to the casual observer making his first visit to the locker room. "There's a silent esprit de corps, as if everyone were thinking good thoughts together," said one visitor.[20]

Lavelle felt that having several born-again Christians on the club improved overall team performance.

"I view it in this way," he told this author. "If you go out and you are performing up to the best of your ability, that's all you can ask of any individual. And to me every time you take the field, that's what you should be doing, is playing up to the best of your ability. You give it all, and then sometimes results are in your favor, sometimes they're not. But it was never because of lack of effort."[21]

Ivie was more effusive, stating in late August 1978, "I think the Christian element on this club is the No. 1 key to our success this year. I just feel that because of our faith, we're able to cope with the problems and pressures easier than most clubs. We feel we are playing for a purpose: to glorify God."[22]

Notes

[1] Duane Sandul, *When Faith Steals Home* (Plainfield, NJ: Logos International, 1980), 93–94.

[2] Duane Sandul, *When Faith Steals Home* (Plainfield, NJ: Logos International, 1980), 96.

[3] Duane Sandul, *When Faith Steals Home* (Plainfield, NJ: Logos

International, 1980), 95.

[4] Glenn Schwarz, "Flying Giants: Sweaty Palms All the Way," *San Francisco Examiner*, June 3, 1979, 33.

[5] William Endicott, " 'Born Again' Ballplayers on Increase," *Los Angeles Times*, August 31, 1979, 19.

[6] Anonymous, "Whitfield One of Pleasant Surprises for SF," June 9, 1977, *The Press-Tribune*, 8.

[7] Albert Morch, "God and the Giants," *San Francisco Examiner*, July 31, 1978, 17.

[8] Duane Sandul, *When Faith Steals Home* (Plainfield, NJ: Logos International, 1980), 99.

[9] Albert Morch, "God and the Giants," *San Francisco Examiner*, July 31, 1978, 17.

[10] Bob Slocum, "God's Squad," *The Modesto Bee*, August 13, 1978, 51.

[11] Duane Sandul, *When Faith Steals Home* (Plainfield, NJ: Logos International, 1980), 100.

[12] Duane Sandul, *When Faith Steals Home* (Plainfield, NJ: Logos International, 1980), 71-72.

[13] Duane Sandul, *When Faith Steals Home* (Plainfield, NJ: Logos International, 1980), 71-72.

[14] Duane Sandul, *When Faith Steals Home* (Plainfield, NJ: Logos International, 1980), 73.

[15] Glenn Schwarz, "Giants Farm Strain, Plank in Final Cuts," *San Francisco Examiner*, April 1, 1979, 35.

[16] Albert Morch, "God and the Giants," *San Francisco Examiner*, July 31, 1978, 17.

[17] Albert Morch, "God and the Giants," *San Francisco Examiner*, July 31, 1978, 21.

[18] Bob Slocum, "God's Squad," *The Modesto Bee*, August 13, 1978, 51.

[19] John B. Koffend, "A Born-Again Giant Hits Harder," *Us*, August 22, 1978, 27.

[20] Albert Morch, "God and the Giants," *San Francisco Examiner*, July 31, 1978, 17.

[21] Gary Lavelle, interview with author, June 1, 2023.

[22] Bob Slocum, "God's Squad," *The Modesto Bee*, August 13, 1978, 51.

Chapter 10
God's Will

If there was one accusation that haunted the God Squadders for years, it was the claim that Knepper, after giving up a game-winning home run, dismissed it as God's will.

Inconsistencies in reporting this charge make it difficult to pinpoint when and where it was supposedly said, and the bulk of the evidence is that Knepper never said it.

For one thing, different accounts attribute the Knepper quote to different years. Without identifying the specific game, in his book, *Playing with God: Religion and Modern Sport*, William J. Baker wrote, "These anxieties [over religion in the locker room] came to the surface in 1978, when San Francisco Giants pitcher Bob Knepper gave up a game-winning home run and reportedly brushed it off as 'God's will.' Knepper denied having made the statement to a reporter, but major league management, players, and media everywhere rushed to debate the issue."[1]

George Vecsey of *The New York Times* said that Knepper made the remark in 1979.[2] On June 1, 1980, a column in the *Dallas Morning News* spoke of "an incident last season when Giant manager Dave Bristol rushed to the mound to throttle pitcher Bob Knepper, who had just given up a home run on an 0-2 pitch. 'Hey, don't blame me,' Knepper said. 'It was God's will.' "[3] The *Napa Valley Register* also said Knepper made the comment during the 1979 season.[4]

Terence Moore, who previously wrote for the *Examiner*

during the God Squad era, stated in a 1989 article for the *Atlanta Journal-Constitution*, "According to a story that circulated during the 1979 winter meetings, Knepper threw a home-run pitch in the bottom of the ninth inning of a game in 1979, and when Giants manager Dave Bristol came to the mound to remove him, the pitcher replied, 'It was God's will.' Neither Knepper nor Bristol remembers that conversation."[5]

But Bristol did not become manager of the Giants, replacing Joe Altobelli, until September 6. 1979. For the remainder of the season, Knepper only pitched two games on the road in which he possibly could have appeared in the bottom of the ninth. But he didn't make it to the ninth inning in either game. In the first game, he gave up home runs to two Cincinnati Reds, both in the first inning. In the second game against the Dodgers, he did not give up any round-trippers.

A *Sports Illustrated* article said Knepper made the statement after he lost a game to the San Diego Padres on June 24, 1980.[6] Art Spander, writing in the *Examiner*, was much less specific, unable to pinpoint the quote. He wrote, "Someplace, sometime during 1980, after he gave up a home run, Knepper was quoted as saying, 'It was God's will.' "[7]

Knepper did indeed give up a game-winning home run on that June date in 1980, when Aurelio Rodriguez belted a two-run shot off the lefty in the eighth inning to give the Padres a 5–3 win. Knepper traces the "God's will" legend to that game. He told the *Santa Rosa Press Democrat*, "It was 1980 and I gave up a home run to a light-hitting third baseman on the Padres that won the game. Dave Bristol came out to the mound and a San Diego writer quoted me as saying, 'It was God's will,' as my explanation to Bristol for giving up the homer. I never said it, but it's followed me along ever since. I became very introverted after that."[8]

The game stories in the two San Diego papers at the time, the *Evening Tribune* and the *Union*, make no mention of the supposed conversation on the mound between Bristol and Knepper. Neither do the game accounts in the *Los Angeles Times* or the *Escondido Times-Advocate*. The San Francisco papers, the *Examiner* and *Chronicle*, also make no note of it.

The most telling evidence that this incident could not have occurred during this game is this part of the *Los Angeles Times* story about the June 24, 1980, game: "The homer was unfortunate for Knepper, whose record sank to 5–9. The lefthander is one of several Giants active as a 'born-again' Christian. He once gave up a homer on an 0–2 pitch and when his manager came to the mound said, in all seriousness, 'I couldn't help it, it was God's will.' "[9]

Unless Knepper was in the habit of saying this any time he gave up a game-losing home run, then he could not have said it in the June 24, 1980, game. The Society of American Baseball Research (SABR) went so far as to claim that Knepper did have this habit. SABR wrote, "When the media would ask Knepper about his performance in the game just pitched, Knepper would say, 'It's God's will.' Unfortunately for the pitcher, he was quoted as saying that when he served up game-losing home runs."[10]

That is a far-fetched claim. The clincher is that Bristol has no remembrance of Knepper ever saying it, nor do any of the managers for whom Knepper played. It is not the type of remark any manager would be likely to forget.

Knepper told this author what transpired after he read the *Los Angeles Times* story:

I chased down the reporter that night [the night after the game] at the ballpark and asked him where he got such a story and was quite adamant with him about him writing a retraction. When I asked him where he came up with that story, he said he read it that previous year at the winter meetings in one of the newspapers there in one of the "quotes" sections some papers used to run. He did not know where it came from other than that . . . a quote attributed to me that I supposedly said about an incident that never happened.[11]

Knepper doesn't know what to make of all the conflicting accounts. In 1981 he told Stan Hochman of the *Philadelphia Daily News*:

There's a story attached to me. When I first saw it, it involved a homer against San Diego. Another version had me giving up a homer on an 0–2 pitch to lose a ballgame. Bristol supposedly asked me what happened. And I supposedly told him it wasn't my fault, it was God's will. I asked Bristol if he ever told anybody that story. He said he couldn't believe anybody would write that.

I talked to the Los Angeles reporter and he said he heard that quote during the winter meetings at Dallas. He never took the time to find out the truth. I happen to be a fanatic about that sort of thing. When I talk to young Christians, I stress that aspect. God gave me X amount of talent. It's God's will that I try to do my best. But if I give up a homer, because I threw a bad pitch, or because the hitter hit a good pitch, I take full responsibility for it.[12]

All of this lends credence to Knepper's insistence that he never said it. As he told sportswriter and baseball historian Mike Sowell in 1995, "That quote followed me around for years, and I never said it. That incident never happened. In fact, I'm very much opposed to that type of theology, that everything that happened in my life was God's will."[13]

If Bristol discussed anything with Knepper when he pulled him from the game after the San Diego home run, it more likely would have been the manager's displeasure with Knepper's pitch selection. The lefty threw Rodriguez a first-pitch fastball, which the third baseman deposited into the seats.

"I reminded Knepper in the middle of the game that he [Rodriguez] is a first-ball, fastball hitter," said Bristol. "So what does he get?"[14]

In July 1980, a month after he gave up the game-winning homer in San Diego, Knepper told the *Chronicle*, "I've never said that God wanted me to throw a home run pitch or make a curveball curve or a fastball faster, as has been reported. I just said that God has made it easier for me to accept things. I haven't become more passive because of it."[15]

But in February 1981, Herb Caen wrote in his column, "The Giants are (or were) plagued by a 'God Squad' of players who didn't mind dropping the ball for an error or striking out with the bases loaded; 'God willed it,' they would explain, simplemindedly."[16]

In April 1981 after the Giants had traded Knepper to Houston, Jim Kaplan of *Sports Illustrated* wrote in a preview of the season, "The Astros are hoping the Knepper of 1981 will be the aggressive fellow who turned in records of 11–9 and 17–11 in '77 and '78, not the God Squad pacifist who slumped to 9–12 and 9–16 and shrugged off every loss as 'God's will.' "[17]

That same month, Knepper told Bill Sullivan of *the Austin American-Statesman*:

> *The version I heard was that I gave up a home run in the eighth, we lost, and I was supposed to have said it was "God's will." The only trouble was that I never said it. You know, there's a tremendous misconception that Christians think that everything that happens is "God's will." Well, as far as I can tell, God never gave up a home run or pitched a shutout. But that stuff stuck with me, and some of the stuff that came out was just incredible.[18]*

However, San Francisco writers kept the unproven accusation alive.

Art Rosenbaum read the *Chronicle's* abridged version of Vecsey's *New York Times* article, which included the statement that Knepper "can neither recall the game nor the quote." Yet Rosenbaum wrote, "A Revival: The God Squad story in the Green [the *Chronicle* sports page] Tuesday morning, in which Gary Lavelle is quoted, 'God does not expect us to be goody-two shoes' and Bob Knepper dismisses a home run off him as 'God's will . . . ' "[19]

Rosenbaum's statement misrepresents what Knepper said in Vecsey's article and serves as another example of how the media spread the unverified "God's will" story.

Art Spander, who read Vecsey's article in the *Times*, wrote two days later of the God Squadders, " . . . the players who deeply believed in their convictions were criticized for their supposed lackadaisical attitudes. According to some, their zeal was put into religion, not baseball. If they went 0-for-4 or got knocked out of the box in the first inning, they indicated it wasn't all that important or that it was 'God's will.' "[20]

The unfounded accusation made its way all the way to Canada. Writing in the Kingston, Ontario, *Whig-Standard*,

Geoffrey Smith stated, "when pitchers Gary Lavelle and Bob Knepper lost in earlier years, they explained it as 'God's will' and told fans 'not to worry.'"[21]

In a 1983 column in the *San Jose Mercury*, Fred Guzman wrote, "You remember the God Squad. Its members constantly praised His name during 1978, when San Francisco spent much of the season in first place, and they said they considered it His will when the team collapsed in 1979."[22]

Knepper told this author, "A couple years later [after the *Los Angeles Times* "God's will" manufactured quote] when I was a player rep for Houston, during our winter player rep meetings, I ran into Scott McGregor of the Orioles. When I introduced myself, he said, 'Oh! You're the guy who said that "Gods will" quote!' Caught me off guard how that story followed me clear into the American League."[23]

The allegation persisted even after all the God Squadders were no longer Giants.

In September 1986, an article in the *Chronicle* began, "A couple of years ago, some Giants were in the habit of crediting wins and losses to divine intervention. As in, 'I guess it was God's will that I gave up those two grand slams.'"[24]

Even Terence Moore, whose writing about the God Squad was fair-minded when he worked for the *Examiner*, penned this diatribe in an article for the *Atlanta Journal-Constitution* in 1987:

> There was also the God Squad, baseball's cliche of cliches. It began during the late 1970s under Joe Altobelli and continued under Robinson. It consisted of Giants pitchers who blamed greater powers for everything from hanging sliders to belt-high fastballs. Among the group's charter members was Bob Knepper, a mellow soul with a magnificent left

arm. He often watched hitters slam one of his sloppy pitches toward Berkeley and say, "It was God's will." In other words, Knepper spent his time with the Giants in a purgatory called apathy. He had company. There were the fans, and there was Johnnie LeMaster, a .200-hitting shortstop whose chief companion was listlessness.[25]

Tim Keown of the *Chronicle* tossed the "God's will" allegation at Lavelle in a 1998 article. Speaking about pitcher Dave Dravecky, Keown wrote: "He arrived after the Giants and the Bay Area had endured 'The God Squad' of the late '70s and early '80s. Players such as Gary Lavelle talked about God imposing his will on a baseball game, making the players mere pawns in a greater battle. The public and the media didn't buy that line of reasoning, which made Dravecky's overt Christianity open to scrutiny."[26]

It is hard not to conclude that the sportswriters were, at best, too lazy to verify the "God's will" accusation, or at worst, biased, in that they continued to spread an allegation about which nobody possessed any evidence. One wonders if they had followed the same practice in writing hard news stories if their subjects would have sued them for libel.

As it turned out, the writers were picking on the wrong guys. If they wanted material to bash the born-again Giants, they should have read the feature story *Us* magazine did on Jack Clark in August 1978. According to the author, John B. Koffend, "In his only time at bat in this year's All-Star Game in San Diego, he was retired on a called third strike. Clark took this Divine Judgment in stride: 'It wasn't His will to let me hit the ball that night.' "

Clark continued, "When I was in the minors, I used to think, 'I'm the best.' I know now I'm not the best. The Lord is the best. He has a purpose and a plan for everybody on this earth. If I go up to the plate and strike out, that's part of His plan for me."[27]

The skeptic would find more ammunition from a statement by Clark after he hit five home runs in four games against Atlanta: "The Lord knew that I had a bad knee and couldn't run out an infield hit. So the Lord blessed my life by letting me hit all those home runs so I wouldn't have to run hard. He was saving my knee."[28]

One might remind the skeptic that Clark had been a born-again Christian less than a year when he made these statements. A more seasoned believer might have noted the difference between claiming a strikeout was God's will and the verse in the New Testament that says, "And we know that God causes all things to work together for good to those who love God, to those who are called according to His purpose."[29] In other words, God can use a strikeout to further develop the character of a Christian, but it doesn't mean that God intended the player to strike out.

The issue of God's will dogged other major league teams in later years. In October 1986, the *Chronicle* reported on dissension over religion in the Seattle Mariners' clubhouse:

> *The Seattle Mariners, the only team in professional baseball that never has had a winning season, have started a campaign to get religion out of the clubhouse.*
>
> *"We have too many [players] who think that if we lose, that's the way the Lord meant it to be," said general manager Dick Balderson, who was in Boston for the World Series. "Changes have to made with the idea that when they come to the park, they will be thinking baseball."*
>
> *Reliever Matt Young agrees. "The thing that has*

bothered me for nearly four years is accepting anything as God's will," Young said. *"When you do something wrong and say that's the way it was meant to be, that's using religion as a crutch. If a guy gets a hit and beats me, I don't say it's the Lord's will, and I've heard that too many times, not just from pitchers,"* he said.[30]

The article included some pushback:

Chuck Snyder, the lay coordinator for the Mariners' chapel, said Balderson "probably fell into the same trap as others do, equating Christianity with weakness." He said, "When they strike out and don't throw their helmet and curse a lot, it may be interpreted that they don't care. But they care. They care desperately."[31]

Mariners first baseman and assistant chapel leader Alvin Davis also disagreed with Balderson. He said, "How do you reach the major league level if you don't care about winning?"[32]

Former Mariner Spike Owen added, "We had a good number of Christian ballplayers on the Mariners; at times we could put a whole Christian team on the field. But that had nothing to do with losing. If anything, being Christian makes a team stronger."[33]

The claim that the born-again Giants passively accepted all outcomes as God's will is inseparable from the accusation that they and other ballplayers lost their competitive edge after becoming Christians.

Is there any evidence to support that theory? Let's see.

Notes

[1] William J. Baker, *Playing with God: Religion and Modern Sport* (Cambridge, MA: Harvard University Press, 2007), 207.

[2] George Vecsey, "Religion Becomes an Important Part of Baseball Scene," *The New York Times*, May 10, 1981, Section 5, 1.

[3] Anonymous, "Hot Stuff," *Dallas Morning News*, June 1, 1980, 59.

[4] Stan Vaughn, "Faith Leads Knepper, Hubbard in Pro Sports Maze," *Napa Valley Register*, April 18, 1981, 6, 8.

[5] Terence Moore, "Baseball and Religion," *Atlanta Journal-Constitution*, August 13,1989, C-1.

[6] Jill Lieber, "Some Say No Leica: Bob Knepper Has a Decidedly Controversial Focus on the World, But His Pitching this Year is Right on Target," *Sports Illustrated*, June 20, 1988, 50.

[7] Art Spander, "Knepper Will Be Judged on Performance," *San Francisco Examiner*, August 6, 1989, 44.

[8] Rich Rupprecht, "Bitter Aftertaste? Not with Knepper," *Santa Rosa Press Democrat*, June 30, 1985, 49.

[9] Mike Granberry, "Rodriguez's Homer Wins It for Padres," *Los Angeles Times*, June 25, 1980, 34.

[10] David E. Skelton, "Bob Knepper," *Society for American Baseball Research*, December 21, 2015, https://sabr.org/bioproj/person/bob-knepper para. 20.

[11] Bob Knepper, interview with author, July 24, 2023.

[12] Stan Hochman, "Knepper Thankful Home is Dome," *Philadelphia Daily News*, October 9, 1981, 122.

[13] Mike Sowell, *One Pitch Away: The Players' Stories of the 1986 League Championships and World Series* (New York, NY: MacMillan, c. 1995), 160.

[14] Glenn Schwarz, "Giants' Woes Continue on Western Trail," *San Francisco Examiner*, June 25, 1980, F-1.

[15] Terence Moore, "The Giants' Bible Brigade," *San Francisco Examiner*, July 27, 1980, 31.

[16] Herb Caen, "Of All Things," *San Francisco Chronicle*, February 12, 1981, 35.

[17] Jim Kaplan, "The West," *Sports Illustrated*, April 13, 1981, 32.

[18] Bill Sullivan, "Bob Knepper: Grand Pitching, Grand Opera," *Austin American-Statesman*, April 30, 1981, D-1.

[19] Art Rosenbaum, "The Plumber Who Became a Star," *San Francisco Chronicle*, May 13, 1981, 71.

[20] Art Spander, "The Giants, God and Satan," *San Francisco Examiner*, May 12, 1981, C-1.

[21] Geoffrey Smith, "Time Out! Where Have All the San Francisco Giants Gone?" *Kingston Whig-Standard*, September 14, 1987, 2.

[22] Fred Guzman, "With Holland Gone, Lavelle Won't Be Left Out this Year," *San Jose Mercury*, March 28, 1983, 78.

[23] Bob Knepper, interview with author, July 24, 2023.

[24] Anonymous, "God Squad the Sequel," *San Francisco Chronicle*, September 10, 1986, 59.

[25] Terence Moore, "Giants Turn from Worst to First in Three Years," *Atlanta Journal-Constitution*, September 27, 1987, D-6.

[26] Tim Keown, "Keeping the Faith," *San Francisco Chronicle*, May 13, 1998, 49.

[27] John B. Koffend, "A Born-Again Giant Hits Harder," *Us*, August 22, 1978, 26–27.

[28] John B. Koffend, "A Born-Again Giant Hits Harder," *Us*, August 22, 1978, 26.

[29] Romans 8:28, New American Standard Bible.

[30] Associated Press, " 'Think Baseball, Not Religion': Mariners Put God on Waivers," *San Francisco Chronicle*, October 25, 1986, 50.

[31] Associated Press, " 'Think Baseball, Not Religion': Mariners Put God on Waivers," *San Francisco Chronicle*, October 25, 1986, 50.

[32] Alvin Davis with Matt Sieger, "The Decision," *Venture*, May/June 1987, 5.

[33] Alvin Davis with Matt Sieger, "The Decision," *Venture*, May/June 1987, 5.

Photo Gallery

The San Francisco Giants' Mike Ivie and Jack Clark embrace during a game against the Los Angeles Dodgers on May 28, 1978, at Candlestick Park. Ivie hit a grand slam in front of the record 56,103-person crowd. (John Storey / San Francisco Chronicle / Polaris)

Jack Clark, dubbed "Jack the Ripper" by Giants teammate Vida Blue, hit 340 home runs and drove in 1,180 runs in his major league career. Clark was a Giant from 1975 to 1984. (@S.F. Giants)

Reliever Gary Lavelle pitched in more games, 647, than anyone in the history of the Giants, including Christy Mathewson (635). He is also first for the franchise in games finished (369) and fourth in saves, with 126. (@S.F. Giants)

Bob Knepper had two stints with the Giants, 1976–1980, and 1989–1990. The teams of both those years were labeled the "God Squad." Knepper's best season as a Giant was 1978, when he went 17–11 with a 2.63 ERA. (@S.F. Giants)

Rob Andrews applies the tag at second base. Andrews played a key role as a utility infielder for the Giants from 1977 to 1979. (@S.F. Giants)

Johnnie LeMaster, who endured booing by the home fans, was actually an excellent defensive shortstop and would have been an even better one if he hadn't played on the notoriously terrible infield at Candlestick Park. (@S.F. Giants)

Mike Ivie hit .308 for the Giants in 1978 and belted four pinch-hit home runs. Two were grand slams, a single-season record he shares with four other major leaguers. (@S.F. Giants)

Terry Whitfield was the model of consistency in his four seasons with the Giants, batting .285 (1977), .289 (1978), .287 (1979), and .296 (1980). (@S.F. Giants)

Hall of Fame catcher Gary Carter played one season, 1990, for the Giants. (@S.F. Giants)

Scott Garrelts played his entire career with the Giants from 1982 to 1991. He led the National League in ERA in 1989 with a 2.28 mark. (@S.F. Giants)

Atlee Hammaker, a key part of the Giants' starting rotation in the 1980s, led the league with a 2.25 ERA in 1983. (@S.F. Giants)

Brett Butler, an expert bunter, played for the Giants from 1988 to 1990 and led the league in runs (109) in 1988 and hits (192) in 1990. (@S.F. Giants)

Jeff Brantley, a Giant from 1988 to 1993, had his best season with the team in 1990, when he posted a microscopic 1.56 ERA with nineteen saves.

Dave Dravecky pitched for the Giants from 1987 to 1989. In addition to his remarkable comeback-from-cancer win at Candlestick Park over the Cincinnati Reds on August 10, 1989, Dravecky pitched a two-hit complete game shutout of the St. Louis Cardinals in Game 2 of the 1987 National League Championship Series. (@S.F. Giants)

Chapter 11
The Killer Instinct

Accusations from the press that the God Squadders were too complacent because of their faith did not begin to surface until the Giants' sub-par 1979 season. Interestingly, little to nothing was written on that score during the team's highly successful 1978 campaign in which the God Squadders played a significant role.

But when hard times fell upon the team, the born-again players were easy marks.

As John Kawamoto wrote in the *Examiner* in 1981:

The so-called "God Squad," the coterie of born-again Christians such as Lavelle, Andrews and former Giants pitcher Bob Knepper, found themselves the subject of several articles by Bay Area sportswriters. More often than not, the articles intimated this inspirational group was a positive force, a reason why the 1978 Giants were able to lead the National League Western division for months. The team ended a respectable third.

But when the Giants staggered to a fifth-place finish [actually fourth-place] in 1979, the catcalls came from both fans and press who described the "Christian Giants" as Bible thumpers who'd contentedly quote Scripture and verse, whether it was after hitting a home run or bobbling a grounder.[1]

Glenn Dickey fired one of the first broadsides on June 11,

1979, when the Giants' record stood at 29–31 and they were 6 ½ games out of first place. He wrote:

> *It should have been obvious that a third-place [1978] team which faded in the stretch and which remained virtually unchanged in the off-season did not have the brightest future. And yet, the Giants strutted around this spring as if they were a cinch for the World Series, the first third-place team I've seen that suffered from over confidence.*
>
> *Why? I suspect one reason is the overabundance of God Squadders on this team. They gave the impression that God would not let them fail. If these players were a little smarter or more sophisticated, they would realize that God takes no special interest in baseball games. Even if He did, there is no reason He should favor the Giants over somebody like Dodger manager Tom Lasorda, who is as public with his piety as any Giants player.*[2]

A couple of readers took issue with Dickey's column. One wrote, "I was very disappointed to read Glenn Dickey's criticism of the Christian members of the Giants. They live by the words of the 'God Squad Manual'—work hard and joyfully, as though you were working for the Lord, and not for your earthly master (Colossians. 3:23). God bless the Giants and forgive Glenn Dickey."[3]

Another wrote, "The Lord has drawn the Giants together so that there is a unity and respect sorely lacking on most teams these days ... Dickey states God does not care about baseball. Has he asked Him? God cares very much for all of His believers."[4]

Dickey was undeterred. By August 13, he was calling for the Giants to trade away some of the God Squadders:

> *The first move the new manager will have to make is to, figuratively, at least, kick the Bibles out of the clubhouse.*
>
> *It may be that the Giants will have to trade one or two of the most obvious born-agains on the club, to break up the clique. At the very least, their lockers should be separated in the clubhouse, and they should be told firmly that their business is playing baseball, not acting as amateur evangelists . . .*
>
> *The problem with this simplistic faith the players have adopted is that it makes them all too comfortable. The born-agains have a tendency to put it all in the hands of the Lord, and the Lord doesn't seem to be pitching too well or hitting in the clutch this season.*[5]

By August 30, when the Giants were hopelessly mired in fourth place with a 59–73 record, seventeen games out of first place, Dickey had become an amateur psychologist:

> *Despite all the strutting and braggadocio, most athletes have very fragile egos, easily shattered. When they do not do as well as they, and others, expect, they cannot handle it.*
>
> *That's the real reason for the upsurge in fundamentalist religion among athletes. Before that, it was psycho-cybernetics and transcendental meditation. There is nothing intellectual about any of this. It's strictly emotional, an attempt to find a way of bolstering one's confidence. But these are only temporary palliatives. When things go wrong, they are of no real help.*
>
> *The latest example of this, of course, is the Giants, As the situation deteriorates, there is more and more finger-pointing. The one thing the players (with the exception of*

Billy North) will not do is look inward, to admit their own mistakes.[6]

At least Dickey's thinking on Christianity and sport was consistent. In October 1978 he wrote a highly controversial piece about boxer George Foreman entitled "Christianity as a Crutch." He stated:

Christianity, of course, is very much in vogue in sports these days. It takes two forms, generally, and I find each form about equally repugnant. The first form is that which we heard so much about from the Giants this last season, in which God is given primary billing., e.g., "God was with me on that last strikeout." . . . The second form of Christianity in sports is the giveup theory. Every event, no matter how bad—is simply treated as God's will, allowing no room for a man to control his own destiny.[7]

Other sportswriters examined the giveup theory. Stephanie Salter wrote in the *Examiner* in May 1980:

There were many writers during the collapse of the '78 Giants season and throughout last year's grim 71–91 season, who indeed did blame the born-againers for the Giants inability to sustain any sort of an attack. The team was referred to as "leading the league in Christers," and the born-again Christians were called "the God Squad."

The theory was that God forgave everything, including losing, and as long as the Christian ballplayers had Jesus to fall back on, what did they care if they had no chance at a National League West division title?[8]

Knepper told Salter he found the theory absurd, stating, "A lot of people don't understand what Christianity is all about. Jesus Christ gave 100 percent in every single thing He did. He never let down. He never dogged it. He was always out there pumping away. He gave me my ability and talent as a big league pitcher, and it would be very wrong not to use that talent."[9]

Lavelle sprang to Knepper's defense.

"They even went as far to imply that Bobby Knepper's faith had made him passive," he said in 1983. "And then reporters wonder why there's a growing tendency for athletes to turn away from the media. It's not fair for the media to make generalizations about Christians, just as it isn't fair for athletes to generalize about reporters."[10]

Knepper told this author:

During that season of 1978, after a game where I did not pitch well, I was asked why I wasn't throwing helmets or bats or having an angry tantrum . . . which caught me off guard because I never did such things ever in my career.

But I had just become a Christian in May of that year. May was the month I was named "Pitcher of the Month," which to me reflected my newfound faith, and my perspective on baseball and life had undergone a change.

To answer the question of why I didn't throw a fit, I should have said, "I never throw a fit," but instead replied that my newfound faith made me more "passive" about bad games. As soon as I used that word, I knew it was the wrong choice of words. But once it was out, some in the media took that and ran with it.

I can remember the next day one of the papers had a headline quoting me saying my faith made me more passive

... again out of context but partly my fault for using that word. What I was trying to convey was that I now was putting a bad pitch or bad game in its proper perspective. I wasn't going to let it destroy my life or my next start or to ruin my confidence etc. God still loved me, my wife still loved me and life would go on. But none of that got explained and instead Christianity made me passive.[11]

That slip of the tongue led to columns like one in November 1978 by Art Rosenbaum, in which he wrote:

I question and have no way of knowing how much the Lord would accept the rationale of born-again athletes who say: If I win, He led me; if I lose, it was His decision that day. Nevertheless, I say that if an athlete — or any person — can find serenity, so be it and God bless you.

Bob Knepper of the Giants was wrestling with a problem last season. He was so immersed in the Lord's good word that he lost aggressiveness, and with it, effectiveness. He seemed to be concluding, though not in direct quotes, that there was a conflict when he merely assigned God all the credit for both victory and defeat.[12]

Knepper did admit that for a short spell, his faith had an adverse effect on his pitching. After the Dodgers knocked Knepper out of the box in the first inning on August 6, 1978, for his fourth straight loss, Glenn Schwarz of the *Examiner* wrote:

Bob Knepper says that becoming a born-again Christian has had a calming effect on his life. Every fifth day, however, the Giants pitcher would not mind a return visit from the jitters he seemed to thrive on during the first half of the season . . .

"By concentrating on not being nervous anymore, I took something that was really good for me as a pitcher and threw it away," Knepper said. "I've become so calm and relaxed, I can't get aggressive anymore. I have to put some fire in my butt."

But Knepper added, "What becoming a Christian has done for me is taught me not to tuck my head between my legs when I lose, I can handle a loss better now."[13]

On September 3, Knepper pitched a complete game, 4–1 victory over the Philadelphia Phillies, his fourth straight win, which followed those four straight losses. He told the *Examiner*, "After I got smoked by the Dodgers, I turned it around with the help of the Lord, Gary Lavelle, and some of the guys. I'm aggressive again now and I feel nervous again before I pitch, which is a good sign. I'm having fun pitching down the stretch."[14]

Don McMahon, the Giants pitching coach in 1980, said during that season, "Bob Knepper can pitch, But sometimes I wish he would be a little more ferocious on the mound. I wish he would keep those hitters a little more concerned about what he's going to do with the ball. But that's not him."[15]

Ralph Wiley of the *Oakland Tribune* wrote of Knepper in 1979, "If Bob Knepper had the menacing disdain of a Sal Maglie [great Giants pitcher of the 1950s], then his easy motion, busting fastball and whirling curve would be . . . there's no telling. But Bob Knepper is not like that and never has been."[16]

But Giant manager Dave Bristol said of Knepper, "Bobby

is a battler. I never thought he was complaisant [sic]."[17]

When the Giants traded Knepper to the Houston Astros in December 1980, Ira Miller of the *Chronicle* wrote:

> *The suspicion, although the Giants wouldn't say it, is that they believe Knepper was never going to be a productive pitcher for them again, that he couldn't handle the pressure of trying to duplicate his '78 season. Knepper himself showed little emotion during his troubled days of the past two years and teammates criticized that seemingly passive attitude, blaming it on his strong religious beliefs.*
>
> *"Because I didn't throw a tantrum, [teammates] thought that I didn't care," Knepper said by phone from his in-laws' residence in Calistoga, Calif.. "It was really hard to hear some of your own teammates think that of you."*[18]

In a column for the *San Jose Mercury* in August 1981 on Mickey Marvin, a born-again Christian football player on the Oakland Raiders, John Lindblom managed to slip in this shot: "Unlike some athletes—former members of the Giants' God Squad, for instance—he doesn't use his religion as a crutch."[19]

Since Lavelle, Clark, and LeMaster were still Giants, it's a good bet that Lindblom was referring to Knepper and Ivie, both of whom had been traded to Houston prior to the 1981 season. If he was including Rob Andrews in his diatribe, Andrews, who retired after the 1979 season, had this answer for the media: "I hate the word 'religion'; it sounds like an organized church activity—as a crutch of sorts to get through life. It is a crutch, but I'd rather be leaning on Jesus than on drugs, or on the shallowness of fame, or fortune, or the 'macho scene.' Everyone has a crutch, whether it's being

'Mr. Workaholic,' a celebrity, or a politician. It's just a choice."[20]

Said Lavelle, "People can always use religion as a crutch. But as far as the Giants' 'God Squadders' are concerned, I don't feel we use it that way. It's just a reality in our lives. The only thing that religion can do is help a person become a better baseball player and a better person all-around. I can't see anything negative about that."[21]

Knepper must have been a man on a mission in 1981. Lindblom changed his tune in his column in the *San Jose Sunday Mercury News* on September 13, 1981:

> *What Bob Knepper has accomplished since the San Francisco Giants traded him to Houston last December is enough to give anybody religion in a hurry. The born-again Christian and one-time mainstay of the Giants' God Squad is now a reborn pitcher for the National League West-leading Astros. And all the questions about whether Knepper was really a competitor—questions which haunted him through his last two seasons with the Giants—have been obscured by five shutouts and a 1.84 earned run average that has to be regarded as competitive by anyone's definition.*[22]

That evening, Knepper proceeded to pitch seven shutout innings against the Giants in the Astrodome to defeat his old team, 3–0.

Asked the difference between his 1981 season in Houston and his two sub-par seasons with the Giants in 1979 and 1980, Knepper told Lindblom, "I think the biggest thing is that no one hassles me anymore about being a committed Christian. I can goof up now and not everyone points at me and says I'm a pacifist."²³

George Vecsey of *The New York Times* interviewed pitcher John Montefusco, who had been a Giant from 1974 to 1980, playing alongside Gary Lavelle all those seasons. "The Count," as he was known, said this:

> *When I was pitching for the Giants, I hated to come out of a game, but I always felt better when Gary Lavelle came in for me. You could see he had competitive spirit. He may hold back his feelings, and maybe that's not healthy, but he is one of the finest people I've ever met in baseball. These are good people. These are my friends. I think the press took a few things and blew it out of proportion to make these guys look bad.*²⁴

After he had retired, Rob Andrews told the *Examiner* in 1981:

> *I don't agree with the statements some columnists made about the group causing apathy. If you're a good Christian, you will try to evaluate, copy, exhibit the qualities that Christ had. If you study Christ's life, you find Jesus gave an effort to anything, regardless of the situation. The "Christian Giants" weren't dogging it. If anything, they were the least likely. I mean, Bobby Knepper has had a couple of rough years pitching, but no one ever accused him of giving up.*²⁵

In a couple of backhanded compliments, because it tarnished other born-again Christians, two *Chronicle* sportswriters admitted that Lavelle was a fierce competitor.

Bruce Jenkins wrote in December 1980:

> There is little left to trade except relief pitching, which brings up Lavelle—and another image problem. Lavelle helped make an organized group out of the Giants' "born-again" religious faction, which has become a hindrance to team performance. Lavelle was always able to maintain his competitiveness—even meanness—on the field, while others could not, and that helps his market value. But when a passive, God-willed-it-that-way attitude becomes dominant in a loser's clubhouse, things become stagnant.[26]

David Bush said this about Lavelle in February 1981: "... unlike some ballplaying Christians, he never has let religion interfere with his performance on the field. He was able to remain competitive—even mean—while pitching."[27]

In 1984 Bill Shirley of the *Los Angeles Times* wrote about Lavelle:

> Gary Lavelle, a born-again Christian who heads the Baseball Chapel for the San Francisco Giants, sees no conflict in his religion and pitching, even when it means having to knock down a batter.
>
> "I believe in protecting my teammates," he said. "There are ways to get across a message. There's no conflict."
>
> Lavelle said he has no problem playing with teammates who cheat to get an edge. "But I don't break the rules," he said. "I don't throw at a hitter; that's wrong. And I've never had a manager tell me to throw at one."[28]

Lavelle said, "I don't know where this passivity rap comes from, because I don't like to lose. And when I don't perform well, I don't say that it's because of his will. That's nothing but a cop-out. The Lord has more important things to worry about than how Gary Lavelle throws a baseball."[29]

Dickey actually put in a good word for Lavelle in a 1979 column after an umpire had ejected the pitcher from a ballgame. He wrote, "The great irony of the ejection from the game in San Diego last week was that umpire Tony Pallone insisted that Lavelle called him a name that cannot be used in a family newspaper. Lavelle has no words in his vocabulary which cannot be used in a family newspaper."[30]

When Dickey stuck to baseball instead of theology, he often was complimentary of Lavelle. In a June 1978 article, Dickey wrote:

> . . . Lavelle was primarily a starting pitcher in the minors. When he came to the Giants, he was converted into a reliever, and that move has made his career — and the Giants. As a short relief man, Lavelle has gotten better and better. He holds the club record for appearances in a season (73) and saves (20) and he has added seven saves and four wins this year in less than a third of the season. More than anybody else, Lavelle kept the Giants out of the cellar the last two seasons, and he has helped to keep them on top of the division this year.[31]

Manager Joe Altobelli came to the born-again Giants' defense. He told Vecsey, "I had no complaint about those guys. Our problem in 1979 was pitching, not our chapel guys."[32]

Speaking with the *Examiner* in 1980, Lavelle remarked:

> We had some bad press, especially last season, because guys naturally start searching for things when you are losing.

And we have some guys on this team who really spoke out about their beliefs when we were going good back in 1978. But basically it's a type thing where the Christians became the scapegoats when we started losing. We're just saying that we want to give 100 percent in whatever we do because that's the way God wants it.[33]

Lavelle elaborated on the theme with this author.

The way the media projected that whole situation, I don't know if they were trying to make headlines with that. I think the thing they tried to project is we were satisfied with just being there. And that was a lie. I think everybody who plays the game at that level is very competitive. I think the other issue, because you didn't use certain language or you didn't rip apart things when you had a rough game or something, that they took that as you didn't care about it. I think [it's] how people perceive certain things. It hurts when you had a bad game just like you rejoice when you had a good one. Nothing ever changed in that regard in my life, anyhow. In my career. I wanted to be the best that I could be.[34]

One teammate told George Vecsey of *The New York Times* off the record that in 1979 he felt some teammates were devoting too much time to prayer and not enough to practice, but added, "We should probably be more like them."[35]

When the Giants were ten games under .500 in early June of 1980, Blue said, "It's hard to put your finger on it, but we just don't have that fight. I don't know if it's the religious thing (the large number of born-again Christians on the club), but we just don't attack the game."[36]

Lavelle told the *Examiner's* Art Spander how he felt about the club's 1979 struggles:

> *People came down hard on us, particularly the press. If they want to label us the God Squad, I don't care as long as that doesn't lead to bad press and bad relations. Some of the things people have written were absolutely untrue. I pray. I think prayer in life is very important. I pray for myself. I pray for other people. But I don't pray to the Lord to pitch no-hitters. I've never said that what happened was "God's will." I believe God gave me a certain ability and he expects me to use that ability to the utmost. I don't believe because I am a Christian I compromise any of my beliefs.*[37]

Ironically, Lavelle played a part in tempering the detrimental fiery nature of a teammate, Tim Foli, who spent the 1977 season with the Giants. According to Dan McGrath of the *Chronicle*, the Giants traded Foli to the Mets after that season because "he had come to be viewed as a maniac in spikes, fighting with umpires, opponents, writers, and, most often, himself."[38]

"I didn't have control of myself," Foli admitted to McGrath. "I used up too much of my energy worrying about the umpires, the fans, other players—things I had no control over."

He said he gained control when he became a Christian, partly due to Lavelle's friendship. He told McGrath in May 1980:

> *I accepted Jesus Christ into my life about two years ago. I'd been raised a Catholic and had gone to Catholic schools, but something was missing in my life. I talked to Gary Lavelle*

about it when I was with the Giants, and in 1978 I went to a Pro Athletes Outreach program in San Diego. That's when I did it. I'm still the same person, but I don't take my shortcomings out on other people anymore, and I try not to worry about things I have no control over.[39]

Regarding his role, Lavelle said, "Tim was a hard-nosed baseball player and I think he was searching when he came over to the Giants. And we ended up having discussions, and you never know. You plant the seeds and God does the harvesting."[40]

Chuck Tanner, Foli's manager on the Pittsburgh Pirates, where Foli arrived in 1979, said, "he'll still do anything he can to beat you."[41]

So would Mark Dewey, a born-again Christian who played for the Giants in 1990, 1995, and 1996. The relief pitcher said:

A lot of times they say that Christian athletes are wimps, that they don't do this or that. But in my opinion, if you're truly walking the walk, as a Christian you ought to be the most unselfish, team-oriented player. You ought to be the guy who works hard, plays hard, does everything he can regardless of whether your team's way out of first. To me, the Christian ballplayer ought to be the guy who breaks up the double play hard and pitches inside, does all the things within the rules of the game, to enhance your chance to win.[42]

As former San Diego Padres pitcher Eric Show noted, "If a Christian pitcher wins 20, his faith is never mentioned. But if he loses 20 the reason given is that he loses because he is a weak, non-competing believer in Jesus."[43]

To the San Francisco sportswriters' credit, when Mike Ivie yo-yoed back-and-forth between retiring and returning to baseball, none accused him of passivity due to his Christian faith. They seemed to understand that Ivie's problem was psychological and emotional, not spiritual. That was in spite of Ivie telling the *Chronicle* when he retired (for a month) in June 1980:

> *There were things I really didn't care for, the traveling, hotels, being away from my family. And playing baseball, I found it tough to lead the walk I wanted to lead with Christ. A lot of moral things, values, didn't coincide with what I believe in. Baseball has given me money and material things I never would have had; it's going to be tough to give up a lot more money. But what it has done to me is distasteful.*[44]

But not distasteful enough to keep him from returning to the Giants three weeks later. Although Ivie said the decisive factor for his return was a phone call from teammate Willie McCovey, he also credited Lavelle, Knepper, and LeMaster, all of whom had learned to navigate whatever conflicts they may have experienced between professional baseball and their faith. Ivie was particularly moved by a conversation with LeMaster.

"Johnnie talked with me the last day of the All-Star break and what he said was inspirational to me," said Ivie. "But what was said between him and me is personal. It's nobody else's business."[45]

Art Rosenbaum wrote about Ivie's short retirement:

> *Mike Ivie, the now-and-then Giants' first baseman, quit the*

game because he thought God didn't want him to fight the pressures of being a professional baseball player. God wanted him to be a normal 9-to-5 man. But, what's normal? Was Ivie talking about something other than baseball per se, like the suggestive language in the locker room or temptations on the road and actions that Jesus would have denounced?[46]

Giant manager Dave Bristol was not as understanding, as Glenn Dickey noted in his column at the end of the 1980 season:

Mike Ivie's career as a Giant is over, if manager Dave Bristol has anything to say about the matter.

"We've got to get rid of the cancer on this club," Bristol told the Chronicle, and he quickly made it clear that getting rid of Ivie would have to be the first step.

"When Ivie cut his hand in the off-season and the doctor told him it would take a year to fully heal, that's all Mike had to hear," Bristol said. "Some players are like that. If you told Roger Metzger it would take two years, he'd say, 'No, it will only take a month.' But Ivie was ready to accept it. The other players know that. When he came back after that 'retirement' and we were on a winning streak, you could just see the air go out of the players."[47]

Ironically, although the Giants traded Ivie to the Astros early in the 1981 season, Bristol never made it that far. Owner Bob Lurie fired him after the 1980 season, and, according to Bristol, one of the reasons may have been his public criticism of Ivie.

Lurie said, "I was certainly not pleased with that. It was

just bad judgment. You [can] have opinions on things, [but there are] certain things you discuss privately."[48]

Ivie would again desert a team, the Houston Astros, departing in August 1981 before the club reinstated him in September.

Commendably, San Francisco sportswriters did not blame it on his Christianity. Art Spander said it best:

> *Mike Ivie can handle a bat but he cannot handle his emotions. Mike Ivie cannot cope. Mike Ivie needs help. That he should be engaged in professional athletics, where problems are magnified, only exacerbates the situation . . . Mike Ivie, unfortunately, is not mentally tough, never has been mentally tough . . . Early on this season the Giants traded him to the Astros. The uniform was different, but the anguish was unchanged. Once more, Mike ran away from reality. One can only express sorrow—and a wish that he will never have to do it again.*[49]

Spander got his wish in May 1983, when the Detroit Tigers released Ivie. He never returned to professional baseball, and he appeared to be the better for it.

The biggest twist in the theory that Christian ballplayers lose their competitive edge came at the expense of Knepper. Ironically, it developed in part because he was overly intent on disproving the theory.

In the 1986 National League Championship Series, Knepper started Game 6 in Houston for the Astros, who trailed in the series, three games to two. The lefty was masterful, limiting the New York Mets to two hits and no runs over eight innings. The Astros led 3–0 as Knepper took the mound in the top of the ninth.

Looking back, Knepper spoke with Mike Sowell about his frame of mind for that critical game:

> *I'm sure I put a lot more pressure on myself because people had criticized a lot of Christian ballplayers for not having that killer instinct. And so I put a lot of Christian ballplayers' reputations on my shoulders that game. I was going to go out and show—and this was probably more subconscious at that time—but I wanted to really go out and pitch and show that a Christian could be the guy in that key situation to have a great game.*[50]

In that fateful ninth, Lenny Dykstra led off with what looked like a playable fly ball to right-center field. But the ball kept carrying, just beyond the reach of Billy Hatcher for a triple. Mookie Wilson followed with a blooper off the handle of his bat toward second baseman Bill Doran, who appeared to not see the ball well, as he took a step or two toward home plate. He leaped and the ball trickled off his glove and onto the outfield grass for a run-scoring single.

Knepper retired Kevin Mitchell on a ground ball, but Keith Hernandez followed with a double, plating Wilson and knocking Knepper out of the game, still clinging to a 3–2 lead. But reliever Dave Smith couldn't hold it, and the Mets tied the game at three-apiece.

The classic battle lasted until the sixteenth inning, when the Mets finally put the game away, 7–6, denying Knepper and the Astros a trip to the World Series.

Knepper reflected on the gut-wrenching loss:

> *In that ninth inning, when I just ran out of gas, or lost a little concentration or whatever happened, that was the*

> *lowest point in my career. Just the way that inning unfolded, I could look back and see an inch here and a fraction of an inch there, and that whole inning changes and we're in the seventh game.*
>
> *It was just a major disappointment for us not to win that ball game. We had worked so hard, and in the playoffs we had come through so many things that just seemed to be against us. And we felt that the Mets had such a psychological thing against trying to hit Mike Scott, who would have pitched Game 7, that if we'd won Game 6, we'd have won Game 7 and we'd be in the World Series.*[51]

The next season, 1987, Knepper lost seventeen games and posted an astronomical 5.27 earned run average. He told the *Port Arthur* (Texas) *News* in 1988, "I never could put it behind me last season. It was such a huge game. Then we lost it and the season ended right there. I shouldered a lot of the blame for it."[52]

Knepper rebounded in 1988, with a 14–5 record and a 3.14 ERA.

Talking with Sowell in 1995, Knepper seemed to have come to terms with that 1986 major disappointment. He said:

> *It really helped put my life in perspective, to realize what's really important in life. Is it winning a game? Is it pleasing people who really don't care about me at all? The majority of the fans and the press, they don't really care about you as a person. All they care about is how you perform for them. So do I want to put that much emphasis on pleasing those people versus pleasing my God?*[53]

It wasn't only the Giants' born-again Christians who were accused of not having the killer instinct.

Terence Moore described the phenomenon:

Cincinnati Reds manager Bob Boone recalled how openly religious players were ridiculed in whispers during the 1970s when he was an All-Star catcher with the Philadelphia Phillies. That was nothing, he said, compared to the time his father, Ray, played in the majors in the late '40s and '50s.

"My daddy was kind of raised that way to bash Christian athletes," Boone said. "Somebody would have a good year and then a bad one after that, and he'd loudly say, 'Oh, that so-and-so player reads the Bible all the time in the clubhouse. He cares more about that than baseball.'

"The miracle is that now my daddy is saved, and so is my whole family," added Boone, who has two sons in the majors. "Unfortunately, I do believe that stigma about Christians being soft still pops up in places."[54]

Basketball Hall of Famer, former New York Knick Willis Reed, had an interesting take on the issue.

"As a Southern Baptist, I prayed before every game of my career," said Reed. "Depending on your background, some guys are competitive, and some aren't, and it doesn't have anything to do with religion."[55]

Notes

[1] John Kawamoto, "Ex-Giant Rob Andrews Reborn as Youth Pastor," *San Francisco Examiner*, April 22, 1981, 75.

[2] Glenn Dickey, "Make a Change, Without Delay," *San Francisco Chronicle*, June 11, 1979, 52.

[3] Chris Canellos, "Letters to the Green: Christianity and the Giants," *San Francisco Chronicle*, June 13, 1979, 44.

[4] Mark Osten, "Letters to the Green: Christianity and the Giants," *San Francisco Chronicle*, June 13, 1979, 44.

[5] Glenn Dickey, "Time to Think About Next Year," *San Francisco Chronicle*, August 13, 1979, 48.

[6] Glenn Dickey, "What Would Really Help the Giants," *San Francisco Chronicle*, August 30, 1979, 61.

[7] Glenn Dickey, "Christianity as a Crutch," *San Francisco Chronicle*, October 12, 1978, 66.

[8] Stephanie Salter, "The Quintessential Bob Knepper," *San Francisco Examiner*, May 25, 1980, 268.

[9] Stephanie Salter, "The Quintessential Bob Knepper," *San Francisco Examiner*, May 25, 1980, 268, 271.

[10] Fred Guzman, "With Holland Gone, Lavelle Won't Be Left Out this Year," *San Jose Mercury*, March 28, 1983, 81.

[11] Bob Knepper, interview with author, July 24, 2023.

[12] Art Rosenbaum, "Is Foreman Really Broke?" *San Francisco Chronicle*, November 7, 1978, 58.

[13] Glenn Schwarz, "Knepper Says He Has Lost His Aggressiveness," *San Francisco Examiner*, August 7, 1978, 47.

[14] Glenn Schwarz, "Giants: 1 Down and 25 to Go," *San Francisco Examiner*, September 4, 1978, 44.

[15] Art Spander, "Knepper Giants' Mystery Man," *San Francisco Examiner*, August 4, 1980, 59.

[16] Ralph Wiley, "Knepper Lacks in Concentration," *Oakland Tribune*, July 5, 1979, 53.

[17] George Vecsey, "Religion Becomes an Important Part of Baseball Scene," *The New York Times*, May 10, 1981, section 5, 1.

[18] Ira Miller, "Giants Trade Knepper for Cabell," *San Francisco Chronicle*, December 9, 1980, 64.

[19] John Lindblom, "Mickey Marvin's Inspiration Comes from Higher Authority," *San Jose Mercury*, August 13, 1981, 89.

[20] John Kawamoto, "Ex-Giant Rob Andrews Reborn as Youth Pastor," *San Francisco Examiner*, April 22, 1981, 75.

[21] Noma Faingold, "Lavelle Answers Critics of 'God Squad,'" *California Aggie*, June 9, 1981, 4.

[22] John Lindblom, "A Heck of a Good Season for Knepper in Houston," *Sunday Mercury News*, September 13, 1981, 53.

[23] John Lindblom, "A Heck of a Good Season for Knepper in Houston," *Sunday Mercury News*, September 13, 1981, 53.

[24] George Vecsey, "Religion Becomes an Important Part of Baseball Scene," *The New York Times*, May 10, 1981, Section 5, 1.

[25] John Kawamoto, "Ex-Giant Rob Andrews Reborn as Youth Pastor," *San Francisco Examiner*, April 22, 1981, 75.

[26] Bruce Jenkins, "Giants' Deals: A Winter of Content," *San Francisco Chronicle*, December 30, 1980, 40.

[27] David Bush, "A Comeback Year in the Giants Bullpen," *San Francisco Chronicle*, February 26, 1981, 63.

[28] Bill Shirley, "There Isn't Any Turning the Other Cheek," *Los Angeles Times*, November 1, 1984, 1.

[29] Fred Guzman, "With Holland Gone, Lavelle Won't Be Left Out this Year," *San Jose Mercury*, March 28, 1983, 81.

[30] Glenn Dickey, "Joe Altobelli Does It Again," *San Francisco Chronicle*, April 13, 1979, 48.

[31] Glenn Dickey, "How to Build a Pitching Staff," *San Francisco Chronicle*, June 7, 1978, 74.

[32] George Vecsey, "Religion Becomes an Important Part of Baseball Scene," *The New York Times*, May 10, 1981, Section 5, 1.

[33] Terence Moore, "The Giants' Bible Brigade," *San Francisco Examiner*, July 27, 1980, 31.

[34] Gary Lavelle, interview with author, June 1, 2023.

[35] George Vecsey, "Religion Becomes an Important Part of Baseball Scene," *The New York Times*, May 10, 1981, Section 5, 1.

[36] Bruce Jenkins, "The Giants Will Deal, If Anyone's Interested," *San Francisco Chronicle*, June 13, 1980, 71.

[37] Art Spander, "The Giants, God and Satan," *San Francisco Examiner*, May 12, 1981, 51.

[38] Dan McGrath, "The Transformation of a Firebrand," *San Francisco Chronicle*, May 15, 1980, 64.

[39] Dan McGrath, "The Transformation of a Firebrand," *San Francisco Chronicle*, May 15, 1980, 64.

[40] Gary Lavelle, interview with author, June 1, 2023.

[41] Dan McGrath, "The Transformation of a Firebrand," *San Francisco Chronicle*, May 15, 1980, 64.

[42] Nancy Gay, "Dewey: Giants' Stalwart Christian," *San Francisco Chronicle*, June 13, 1996, D-5.

[43] Lori Rotenberk, "Pray Ball—An Inside Look at Rising Legion of Baseball Bible Belters," *Chicago Sun Times*, August 22, 1988, 1.

[44] Glenn Schwarz, "Ivie Retires, and Giants Ask—Why?" *San Francisco Examiner*, June 26, 1980, 51.

[45] Glenn Schwarz, "Ivie Retires, and Giants Ask—Why?" *San Francisco Examiner*, June 26, 1980, 51.

[46] Art Rosenbaum, "Good and Evil Among Sports Personalities," *San Francisco Chronicle*, July 9, 1980, 59.

[47] Glenn Dickey, "Bristol Set to 'Dump' Ivie," *San Francisco Chronicle*, October 17, 1980, 75.

[48] Ira Miller, "Why Was Bristol Fired? Only Bob Lurie Knows," *San Francisco Chronicle*, December 10, 1980, 73.

[49] Art Spander, "Ivie's Sad Battle with Reality," *San Francisco Examiner*, August 12, 1981, 63.

[50] Mike Sowell, *One Pitch Away: The Players' Stories of the 1986 League Championships and World Series* (New York, NY: MacMillan, c. 1995), 161.

[51] Mike Sowell, *One Pitch Away: The Players' Stories of the 1986 League Championships and World Series* (New York, NY: MacMillan, c. 1995), 162.

[52] Tom Halliburton, "Knepper's Hard Work Does Not Go Unrewarded," *Port Arthur News,* July 10, 1988, 10.

[53] Mike Sowell, *One Pitch Away: The Players' Stories of the 1986 League Championships and World Series* (New York, NY: MacMillan, c. 1995), 166.

[54] Terence Moore, "The God Squad: Many Pros Keep Faith in Play All Week," *Atlanta Journal-Constitution*, August 5, 2001, A-1.

[55] Terence Moore, "The God Squad: Many Pros Keep Faith in Play All Week," *Atlanta Journal-Constitution*, August 5, 2001, A-1.

Chapter 12
Jesus at the Bat

When a ballplayer brings Jesus into his life, can it improve his performance? One could look at batting averages and ERAs before and after a player became a Christian to try to answer the question. But too many other factors can affect those statistics. Increased experience in the big leagues can lead to improvement. Conversely, age can lead to decline. Even something as simple as a change in one's slot in the batting order can impact a player's statistics for a season.

So the only source to test the theory is the player himself. Admittedly, the player's opinion could be biased. But let's hear what the ballplayers had to say.

Scott Garrelts, who pitched for the Giants from 1982 to 1991, became a born-again Christian in 1984. Primarily a reliever in his first seven seasons with the Giants, he was promoted to the starting rotation in 1989, when he led the league in ERA with a 2.28 mark and posted a 14–5 record. He credited his faith for his success.

> *Throughout my minor league career, I always felt like I was a .500 pitcher. I'd win a game, lose a game, win two, lose two—because I always had that feeling that I'm going to lose. It wasn't until I got into the major leagues that I realized that God doesn't want you to lose. He wants you to be successful. And it wasn't until I realized that, that I was able to overcome the fear of being a .500 pitcher and to excel*

and to be more than that. It helped me not to think on the negative things. It helped me concentrate on what I had to do.[1]

Catcher Mike Matheny, who played for the Giants in 2005 and 2006 and went on to manage the St. Louis Cardinals and the Kansas City Royals, sounded a similar theme, telling this author that he had such a dreadful spring training before his first season with the Cardinals in 2000 that he worried he wouldn't make the cut.

"My walk with God was as strong as it had ever been," he said, "but my baseball was terrible."

He spent a lot of time in prayer, talked with his wife, Kristen, and came to realize the problem.

"I had been playing not to fail," he explained, noting that he was too concerned about making his new team. He dove back into baseball with new boldness. He not only made the team but was the starting catcher on opening day and went on to win his first Gold Glove.[2]

Another catcher, Gary Carter, who joined the Giants for one season in 1990, shared with this author his thoughts about the relationship between faith and performance. In Game 6 of the 1986 World Series, Carter's Mets were one out away from losing the series, four games to two, to the Boston Red Sox. Boston led 5–3 as New York batted in the last of the tenth inning. With two outs and nobody on, Carter came to the plate.

"I felt that God was going to bat with me," he said. "I felt so confident."[3]

He lined a base hit into left field. The next two Mets also got hits. Then, after a wild pitch allowed the tying run to score, Mookie Wilson hit a ground ball that went through the legs of Red Sox first baseman Bill Buckner, giving the Mets a 6–5 victory. New York went on to win Game 7 and become the World Series champions.

Carter said it was not unusual for him to feel that God was with him as he went to bat. In fact, he enjoyed the pressure situations.

"I just pray in my heart about it," he said. "Then I go up there, and I feel like He gives me something extra."[4]

After retiring from baseball, Carter elaborated in 1997 on his at-bat that inning:

> *While in the on-deck circle, I really felt the presence of God right there. I normally prayed while in the on-deck circle, but this time I prayed maybe just a little more. With divine intervention, I was able to line a base hit into left field, which led to a rally and our winning the game 6–5. We then won Game 7 and the World Series. Without God in my life, that moment may have never happened. With God, I felt I was the best ballplayer I could be.*[5]

The Hall of Fame catcher, who died at age 57 in 2012 from brain tumors, added, "As athletes, we're blessed with the ability to play the game. If you're able to look in the mirror and say, 'Hey, I gave it my very best,' it's between you and God. And if you're shortchanging yourself, you're the one to blame. So I've always taken that out on the field every day, and it's made me a better ballplayer. Because I don't ever try to underachieve. I always try to overachieve."[6]

After a successful 1976 season in which Gary Lavelle went 10–6 with twelve saves and a 2.70 ERA, he told Glenn Schwarz of the *Examiner*:

> *There's no doubt the Lord helps me in all aspects of life. I ask Him and He helps me. The most important thing is to give all the glory to Jesus . . . everything I do is His. Like, He eliminated fear from my life. Now, when I'm pitching, I think positive and no longer think I'm going to get beat. I read the Bible every day for at least half an hour and I always think on this one passage from the book of Philippians. It says, "I can do all things through Christ who strengthens me."*[7]

When Lavelle got off to a bad start in 1980, the Giants replaced him with Al Holland as the short-inning, left-handed reliever and relegated Lavelle to middle relief. He talked about it with Stephanie Salter of the *Examiner* before the beginning of the 1981 season. She wrote:

> *Pitching coach Don McMahon theorizes that Lavelle's old form, like that of many pitchers, was based on aggression and what McMahon terms being "pleasantly wild."*
>
> *"The same thing happened to the Count," McMahon said of former Giant John Montefusco. "He got older and he got control. Batters know that Gary's involved with the Christian athletes thing and that he's a nice guy. He's got to just run it in on them a little bit. You don't have to hit anybody, but you need that little wildness."*
>
> *Lavelle, as might be expected, doesn't fully agree. "I think aggressiveness is overrated," he said. "I come in on guys when I have to. The day I lose my aggressiveness is the day I'll probably have to quit. But I've been pitching seven years now in the majors and my style is the same as it's always been."*[8]

Lavelle went on to discuss how he had adjusted to middle relief. But, lest anyone think his Christianity made him content to stay in that role, he concluded:

Hey, I don't plan to be rejoiceful as a middle reliever. I'm confident that I can get back to what I enjoy doing most. This is something you have to expect and adjust to, that's what pitching is. If you don't go crazy and can keep your confidence and sanity and drive, you can make it. I've got a lot of good years left and I want to be the best there is. I don't ever want to lose that.[9]

Lavelle had an outstanding season in 1982 and regained his role as closer in 1983.

In August 1978, Bob Knepper told *Us* magazine, "Ten days before I became a Christian, my throwing rhythm was way off. Then I thought of tucking my right elbow inside my knee in the windup, and it worked. I shut out Houston that night, 1–0. But it was only much later that I realized that God had spoken to me. It wasn't my idea, it was His."[10]

Truth be told, it might have been Vida Blue's idea. After that 1–0 shoutout of the Astros on May 30, 1978, Knepper told the *Chronicle*, " . . . It wasn't until Vida came here that I picked up one more thing. He keeps his right elbow inside his leg when he delivers the ball. I'd always held it outside and it would get in the way when I threw. Tonight I changed over for the first time, and I felt unbeatable."[11]

To be charitable, one might infer that Knepper was reminded, perhaps by God, of what he had seen Blue do. In any case, it worked.

Nick Peters of the *Sporting News* wrote this about Jack Clark:

Ask Jack for the main reason behind his change of attitude and impressive statistics in 1978 and he doesn't hesitate to answer.

"I've accepted God," he said. "I wasn't getting fulfillment out of baseball last year, so I turned to the Lord and let Him guide me. I enjoy telling people about my involvement with the Lord and how He blesses my life. I find some people turn around and walk away when I start talking about it. But that's their problem."[12]

In July 1979 Clark told the *Santa Cruz Sentinel*:

Earlier in the year, I was putting a lot of pressure on myself, wanting to be the one to turn it all around for us. I was trying too hard to get the big hit and, as a result, I was hurting the club more than helping it. I just had to learn to relax when going up to the plate. That's something I pray about—for the Lord to help me and show me the answer and give me strength.[13]

Art Rosenbaum addressed the question of whether Christian ballplayers can play aggressively when he interviewed Rob Andrews in August 1979:

He believes in Christ with a passion but, he says, his new-found direction has made him (and others of the squad) even better baseball performers. Such an assertion is open to argument because, with the Giants' downfall, some observers searching for faults have decided it's all due to a lack of aggressiveness—that excessive serenity, if such a state is possible, is derived from believing God will take care of everything . . .[14]

Andrews, who had been the starting second baseman, told Rosenbaum that his faith helped him to adjust to the role of utility player after the Giants benched him and shifted Bill Madlock from third base to second base:

"I began to work at learning to give of myself by practicing hard, encouraging the team on the bench . . . ," he said. "I was experiencing joy and peace such as never before. And when I had a chance to play, God blessed my performance."

Rosenbaum concluded, "Are baseball performances blessed? Ask God. He knows."

Giants manager Joe Altobelli told *Us* magazine in 1978, "What Christianity does, I think, is unload some of the burdens a man can carry out to his position. Christianity makes things weigh less."[15]

Mark Dewey, who played a key role out of the bullpen for the Giants in 1996, pitching in seventy-eight games, said, "I don't base my season on my statistics. I pray that I will concentrate, be intense, and use the ability God has blessed me with. I also base my success on how I've enhanced the chances of the team winning. I've never had a year anywhere where I think my value to the team has been greater than it was that season [1996]."[16]

Jim Reeves of the *Fort Worth Star-Telegram* asked Texas Ranger catcher Jim Sundberg in 1981 if his commitment to Jesus helped his performance and received a ringing endorsement:

> *I think the record speaks for itself. Before I accepted Christ [in 1977], I was a .228 hitter in the big leagues. Since then I'm a .282 hitter. Before, I'd won one Gold Glove. Since then I've won four more.*
>
> *It's helped me to relax and be more confident. I know*

that, professionally as a player, I would have done better because of maturity, growing stronger and other natural factors, but as far as progressing like I have, I believe my faith has been a key factor. In fact, I feel that as I get deeper into my faith, I should become better because it'll help me to deal with the inefficiencies and problems that I have now.[17]

There are times, however, when it probably would be better for a born-again player to remain silent. In June 1985, the *Omaha World-Herald* reported:

St. Louis Manager Whitey Herzog has stuck with catcher Darrell Porter, who has yet to throw out a would be base stealer. But when Porter took 10 fastballs while striking out four times the other night, Herzog told Porter, "Darrell, you've got to do better than that."

A born-again Christian, Porter reassured Herzog that the Lord was with him.

"You better listen to me," Herzog replied. "The Lord's a terrific guy, but he doesn't know anything about hitting."[18]

Glenn Dickey did not think God took any particular interest in athletic performance, writing, "Religion and sports have made strange, but persistent, bedfellows over the years. There is a certain arrogance in this, of course, the implication being that God is watching the games, presumably from a seat on the 50-yard line or a box behind first base."[19]

Lowell Cohn had a humorous take on the issue. In May 1980 he wrote:

I was browsing through the Sporting News last week when

I came upon the following headline: "Foster Finds Faith a Positive Factor." The article tells how George Foster of the Cincinnati Reds first noticed a change in himself when he went to a hypnotist. . . . the article goes on, "the biggest change in Foster . . . came when he 'took God into my life.' "

Some guys get every edge. Not only is Foster one of the most awesome power hitters in baseball, not only does he regularly pump up his already mighty muscles with weights, not only does he consult a hypnotist—but, now we find out he also has God on his side. It hardly seems fair. Ordinary guys like Darrell Evans and Marc Hill could use a little help from the deity just to nudge their averages above .250—how else are they going to do it? Superstars like Foster ought to have the good taste to go it alone.[20]

Hall of Fame manager Sparky Anderson expressed his skepticism in an interview with *Playboy* in 1985:

"So many baseball teams have their 'God Squads' these days," said Anderson, "players who after they hit a home run credit God with their good swing . . . like, 'God made me hit that home run.' You hear that a lot these days. I look at it this way: If God let you hit a home run last time up, then who struck you out next time at bat?"[21]

Bill Madlock put it in perspective, telling reporter Bob Slocum during the 1978 season, "It's sort of misleading to say, 'Well, because we have this Christian element on the club, we are winning.' I think our faith helps us handle situations more effectively and helps us to play to our capabilities, that's all."[22]

Notes

[1] Matt Sieger, "Scott Garrelts: Making it in the Majors," *Teen Quest*, March 1991, 38.

[2] Mike Matheny, interview with author, May 2005.

[3] Matt Sieger, "Gary Carter is Not Shy," *Teen Quest*, November 1991, 29.

[4] Matt Sieger, "Gary Carter is Not Shy," *Teen Quest*, November 1991, 31.

[5] Dave Brannon, *Safe at Home 2* (Chicago: Moody Press, 1997), 12.

[6] Matt Sieger, "Gary Carter is Not Shy," *Teen Quest*, November 1991, 31.

[7] Glenn Schwarz, "Lavelle and the Lord," *San Francisco Examiner*, May 29, 1977, 33.

[8] Stephanie Salter, "Bible Helps Giants' Lavelle Adjust to Long Relief," *San Francisco Examiner*, March 29, 1981, 36.

[9] Stephanie Salter, "Bible Helps Giants' Lavelle Adjust to Long Relief," *San Francisco Examiner*, March 29, 1981, 36.

[10] John B. Koffend, "A Born-Again Giant Hits Harder," *Us*, August 22, 1978, 27.

[11] Bruce Jenkins, "Knepper Beats Astros, 1-0, on Five-Hitter," *San Francisco Chronicle*, May 31, 1978, 51.

[12] Nick Peters, "Clark Complete, Confident . . . and only 22," *The Sporting News*, August 19, 1978, 8.

[13] Alan Arakelian, "Clark Keeping the 'Faith' in Life," *Santa Cruz Sentinel*, July 1, 1979, 56.

[14] Art Rosenbaum, "The Lord and Rob Andrews," *San Francisco Chronicle*, August 28, 1979, 50.

[15] John B. Koffend, "A Born-Again Giant Hits Harder," *Us*, August 22, 1978, 27.

[16] Dave Brannon, *Safe at Home 2* (Chicago: Moody Press, 1997), 84.

[17] Jim Reeves, "Dugout Religion," *Fort Worth Star Telegram*,

February 8, 1981, 37.

[18] Steve Pivovar, "A.L West Catching Up with Big Bad East," *Omaha World-Herald*, June 2, 1985, 2.

[19] Glenn Dickey, "Praise the Lord and Hit to Right," *San Francisco Chronicle*, November 15, 1976, 46.

[20] Lowell Cohn, "Can Satan Save the Giants?" *San Francisco Chronicle*, May 7, 1980, 72.

[21] Ken Kelley, "Losin' is Lousy," *Playboy* interview, published in *Detroit Free Press*, April 28, 1985, 42.

[22] Bob Slocum, "God's Squad," *The Modesto Bee*, August 13, 1978, 51.

Chapter 13
Satan and the Giants

Lowell Cohn did not write many columns about the God Squadders. He was a columnist, not a beat writer, so he wasn't in the Giants' clubhouse every game. Besides, he had to also write about the San Francisco 49ers, the Oakland Raiders, the Golden State Warriors, and the Oakland A's.

But when he did approach the topic, he did it with gusto.

Cohn, who earned a PhD in English literature at Stanford University, never went to journalism school. When he landed an opportunity to work as a sports columnist for the *San Francisco Chronicle* in November 1979, he wanted to make an immediate impression.

"I took strong stands because that's just how I was," he wrote. "And I needed to make a splash. Needed to keep my job. I was on a six-month trial, and if I were mere background noise, the *Chronicle* would drop me in a second."[1]

He told this author that was his frame of mind when he produced his column, "Can Satan Save the Giants?" on May 7, 1980. And it made quite a splash.

On the day the *Chronicle* published the column, the Giants were in last place in their division with an 8–18 record. In his satirical piece, Cohn concluded that God must hate the Giants. He wrote:

> *But what does he have against our local heroes? He's downright prejudiced against them. No question about it. He has*

them so befuddled they can't even count the outs. The irony in all this is that the Giants are a God-fearing bunch if there ever was one. I'll bet, prayer for prayer, they're the most God-fearing team in major league baseball. It's not for me to say why God has singled out the Giants—His ways are very mysterious to man. But as long as things are already shot to hell, I have a suggestion. Join the other team, fellas. Throw in with the Prince of Darkness—the Big D.[2]

Cohn went on to recommend that at least one Giant sell his soul to the devil to turn the team's season around, just as long-suffering Washington Senators fan Joe Boyd did in the novel, *The Year the Yankees Lost the Pennant*, the inspiration for the 1955 musical comedy, *Damn Yankees*, which in turn generated the movie of the same name (Joe Boyd was renamed Joe Hardy for those productions).

"I was joking around," Cohn told this author. "I wrote my satire on the soul because that's what people were talking about. Glenn [Dickey] had written about it. I wasn't accusing them. I was just trying to have fun."[3]

But, as he would soon discover, some of the Giants didn't get the joke.

In mid-June, the Giants, ten games under .500, were in New York to play the Mets, and Cohn made the rookie journalist mistake of catching a forty-five-minute ride on the team bus from the Giants' hotel in Manhattan to Shea Stadium in Queens. He didn't know that no ballplayer wants a sportswriter on the team bus. Cohn says he never rode the team bus again.

But this time he did and was standing, while most of the players were sitting. Cohn, who had been critical of the Giants, as had other Bay Area writers, told this author:

John Montefusco was in the back. He didn't like me at all. So he started yelling at me. It's more than 40 years ago, but I think he said one, "F___ you, Lowell!" The bus stopped at a light in Manhattan. There was a homeless person on the street, and Montefusco yelled, "See that f___in' bum, that's Lowell's brother!"

I was still standing up. It happened very quickly. There happened to be an empty seat next to Johnnie LeMaster. He grabbed me and said, "Sit down here, I'll take care of you." LeMaster was one of my all-time favorite athletes I ever covered. He is the most decent, lovely person.

But he was troubled, and he said to me, "Why did you write we should sell a soul to the devil?" And I said, "Johnnie, I didn't mean it. It was satire." And Johnnie, in the goodness of his heart, said, "What's satire?" And I'm not putting him down. I love Johnnie. He just didn't know. And I tried to explain, you're making a joke, and I don't think I ever adequately explained it to Johnnie. But the point was, even though he disapproved of what I had done, he didn't disapprove of me. And he protected me from what he saw as a verbal onslaught from Montefusco. And by the way, I don't have any hard feelings toward Montefusco. God love John Montefusco. I'm telling you what happened like 43 years ago.[4]

Cohn related the second half of the story:

So now we get to Shea Stadium, and I already have a migraine headache because of what happened on the bus. So I'm in the dugout and now Vida Blue—and I didn't really even know Vida Blue—comes up and he doesn't know how to pronounce my name, which is Cohn [like Cone]. And he says, "Are you Lowell Cun?" I said yeah. and I thought, I've already got a migraine and now this, I've got to deal with Vida Blue.

On the contrary. There are all these guys in the dugout. He puts his arm around me and says, "Lowell Cun, you're okay by me," letting everybody know, "Don't screw with this guy." Then he explained, "Lowell Cun, I like the God Squadders. But I think they feel losing is God's will, and it troubles me."

Vida objected to them. He liked them. How could you not? They were nice guys. But he felt they had a fundamental disagreement. Vida did not accept losing, and I'm not saying they did. It was his perception of them, that they thought losing was God's will And he wanted everybody to know he approved of the guy, me, who questioned that.[5]

Cohn added that he did not share Blue's perception because no born-again Giant ever said anything like that to him.

"I felt that Gary Lavelle, for example, was a kickass competitor," said Cohn. "Absolutely. And Johnnie [LeMaster] as well. I was a columnist, so I would drop in and out. I'm not there every day the way a beat writer is. But I dropped in thousands of times, and I never, ever heard a player say that."[6]

Almost a year to the day after "Can Satan Save the Giants?" Cohn wrote a sequel, "Lavelle and the Fiend," inspired by the piece by George Vecsey of *The New York Times* that appeared in the *Chronicle* on May 12, 1981, under the title, "How God Affects the Giants." Vecsey quoted Lavelle as saying, "One columnist wrote we were not getting anywhere by praying to Jesus and that maybe we should try praying to Satan. I remember that column well. I was not really surprised. The Bay Area is the center of devil worship, radical groups and homosexuality in this country. It is a satanic region."[7]

Lavelle responded to Vecsey's column, telling the *Examiner's* Art Spander:

> *There is a spirit of evil, a satanic spirit influencing the area. I mean that from a spiritual level. That doesn't make the majority of people in the Bay Area bad. It just means that there are forces working on people which may influence them incorrectly. There is a large homosexual population in the Bay Area. I can't condone homosexuality. But if a homosexual came to me for help, I would do my utmost to help him. The spiritual problems do not make people evil by any means. I just do not condone the way many people live.*[8]

He explained to the *California Aggie* in June 1981, "The question that was originally asked by the New York writer [Vecsey] was, 'Why do you think the Bay Area papers were so negative toward the God Squad?' I feel this is a strong satanic region, meaning in the spiritual sense. My purpose for saying that was I feel as a Christian that this area is under strong spiritual oppression. There is an actual church of Satan in San Francisco."[9]

Lavelle elaborated in an interview in March 1983 with *San Jose Mercury* columnist Fred Guzman:

> *The point I was trying to get across, and which the writer [Vecsey] ignored, was that there are more temptations in baseball than in most other areas of society. The money, the travel, and the exposure athletes receive can have a negative*

effect on a person. But after you've been around the game for as long as I have, you realize that money, fame and women—all the things we regard as good—do not provide a person with true happiness. Peace comes from within a person.[10]

The day after the Vecsey column appeared in the *Chronicle*, Cohn published "Lavelle and the Fiend." Recognizing that in the Vecsey article Lavelle was referring to Cohn's "Can Satan Save the Giants?" column, the ever-satirical Cohn wrote, " . . . Lavelle says he remembers my column well. Not true . . . I suggested they sell a soul to the devil, not just pray to him. I'm sure you'll admit there's a big difference."

Cohn continued:

For a guy who preaches religious tolerance, [Lavelle] is guilty of intolerance. He's intolerant of radicals, homosexuals and the Bay Area . . . There are tens of thousands of homosexuals in the Bay Area, especially in San Francisco, but I've talked to some of those homosexuals and they say they always thought Gary Lavelle was a good guy and that they rooted for him when he came into the ballgame. Now I'll bet they'll change their attitude.

In conclusion, composing his own tongue-in-cheek version of "Sympathy for the Devil," Cohn wrote, "Lucifer also made appearances in 'Damn Yankees,' 'The Devil and Daniel Webster,' 'Rosemary's Baby,' and 'The Exorcist.' In each case, I am told he went over real big. So I don't know what Gary Lavelle's problem is. Maybe I do. When it comes to religion, Gary Lavelle doesn't have the least particle of a sense of humor."[11]

Once again, his column had repercussions with the Giants. He wrote about it nine days later in a column titled "Friendly Persuasion." He had wandered into the Giants' clubhouse when LeMaster called him over. He was expecting LeMaster to rake him over the coals for his "Lavelle and the Fiend" column. Instead, Cohn wrote that LeMaster asked him, without a trace of anger, "What do you have against religion?' Cohn wrote:

> *Like Lavelle, LeMaster is a born-again Christian. To them, Satan is no metaphor of evil, but a foul fiend who mingles with us and poisons our world. This never has been easy for me to take seriously . . . I thought LeMaster would drop to his knees and pray for me right there. He lapsed into silence. We had always gotten along well, and now I had turned out to be an alien being. The air was not tense, only sad.*[12]

After LeMaster informed Cohn that Lavelle had received some nasty letters in response to his column, Cohn walked over to Lavelle, who was dressing in front of his locker. Cohn asked if Vecsey had misquoted Lavelle. Lavelle replied:

> *No. But my answers sounded different when you didn't hear the questions also. I saw where you wrote I don't have a sense of humor about religion. It's true. How can I joke about damnation? People go to hell, you know. God says they do. That's very serious. And God says homosexuality is a sin. You have to understand this. I condemn the sin, not the sinner. I still have friends who are homosexuals. I'm their friend, but I tell them God says it's a sin.*[13]

Cohn concluded by confessing his frustration that neither LeMaster nor Lavelle had gotten upset with him:

> *The theology of LeMaster and Lavelle seemed so primitive to me—this taking Satan and the Garden of Eden literally, and seeing sexual preference in terms of "sin." . . . Even if I thought some of their beliefs were wacko, I had to admit LeMaster . . . and Lavelle were patient and kind, and had even turned the other cheek. If they had been conspirators, they couldn't have made things more difficult for me.*[14]

Regarding turning the other cheek, Lavelle told this author, "I think God calls us to do that, and he's [Cohn] going to do what he's going to do, so I'm not going to feed more fuel to the fire by doing something God says I shouldn't do. I do remember him coming up and we talked about that. I don't remember the whole discussion."[15]

How did Lavelle feel about Cohn's contention that he was intolerant? He replied:

> *The way I would respond to that, and I believe this is what I said to him, [is] God loves the sinner, not the sin. And that's how I feel. I don't judge homosexuals. They've got to face God. But I go by what the Bible tells me, the Word of God. It doesn't mean I'm intolerant. It just means I don't believe the same way they do. And he took that and wrote that the way that it made me seem like I just hated the homosexuals and all that stuff, which wasn't true . . . If the context of the question was, did I hate homosexuals, I would have answered no.*
>
> *So I think when you make a statement like that to write an article to make you famous or whatever, that to me—I*

used to get death threats from that article—what he had said was totally taken out of context. And I also said the Church of Satan was started in San Francisco by Anton LeVay [Vecsey did not include that in the article]. That's just fact. That's not hearsay. And I said from a spiritual aspect, I think it's [San Francisco] very oppressed spiritually—nothing else—spiritually. And I've never held any grudges against Glenn Dickey or Lowell Cohn. In fact I prayed for them. Everybody has to walk to the beat of their own drum and everybody is going to answer to God one day. And I'm not the judge.[16]

Cohn told this author:

I do remember the original satire ["Can Satan Save the Giants?"], but I don't remember those ["Lavelle and the Fiend" and "Friendly Persuasion."] But as you read it to me, I was hoping that I came through, that I didn't put them down. Because I was a young man and sometimes I was precipitous in my reactions. But I'm glad I came through, and they deserved it.

    As I was listening to you go over the final two columns, I realized I called it primitive. I probably wouldn't use that adjective now. Clearly Johnnie and Gary, at the time and maybe still, believe in hell and believe in the devil. I certainly don't. I think they're metaphors. I'm not saying I'm right and Gary is wrong. We have different views. It's faith, it's not intellectual, it's from your emotions, it's from your gut. So I wish I had not used the word primitive. I was a young man. I would have explained it the way I just explained it to you.[17]

Notes

[1] Lowell Cohn, *Gloves Off: 40 Years of Unfiltered Sportswriting* (Petaluma, CA: Roundtree Press, 2020), 13.

[2] Lowell Cohn, "Can Satan Save the Giants?" *San Francisco Chronicle*, May 7, 1980, 72.

[3] Lowell Cohn, interview with author, May 23, 2023.

[4] Lowell Cohn, interview with author, May 23, 2023.

[5] Lowell Cohn, interview with author, May 23, 2023.

[6] Lowell Cohn, interview with author, May 23, 2023.

[7] George Vecsey, "How God Affects the Giants," *San Francisco Chronicle*, May 12, 1981, 45.

[8] Art Spander, "The Giants, God and Satan," *San Francisco Examiner*, May 12, 1981, 51.

[9] Noma Faingold, "Lavelle Answers Critics of 'God Squad,'" *California Aggie*, June 9, 1981, 4, 6.

[10] Fred Guzman, "With Holland Gone, Lavelle Won't Be Left Out this Year," *San Jose Mercury*, March 28, 1983, 81.

[11] Lowell Cohn, "Lavelle and the Fiend," *San Francisco Chronicle*, May 13, 1981, 67, 69.

[12] Lowell Cohn, "Friendly Persuasion," *San Francisco Chronicle*, May 22, 1981, 86.

[13] Lowell Cohn, "Friendly Persuasion," *San Francisco Chronicle*, May 22, 1981, 86.

[14] Lowell Cohn, "Friendly Persuasion," *San Francisco Chronicle*, May 22, 1981, 86.

[15] Gary Lavelle, interview with author, June 1, 2023.

[16] Gary Lavelle, interview with author, June 1, 2023.

[17] Lowell Cohn, interview with author, May 23, 2023.

Chapter 14
Understanding Lowell Cohn

Lowell Cohn played a key role in the God Squad controversy. A New York Jew from Brooklyn, he was not the typical Bay Area sportswriter.

In the introduction to his book, *Gloves Off: 40 Years of Unfiltered Sportswriting*, he wrote that he "took controversial stands, criticized local teams when they deserved it. Not the norm in the Bay Area, where sports writers were considered soft, especially compared to the blunt plainspoken, in-your-face style of New York City, where I was from and where I learned to think and talk and write."[1]

Brian Murphy, the popular Bay Area sports-radio host who also covered sports for the *San Francisco Chronicle* for fifteen years, said this about Cohn:

> You'd never meet a less-stuffy guy with a literature doctorate than Lowell Cohn. That's what makes Lowell's writing so great. Take a big brain that's read all the great books, add in an innate passion for sports, combine it with a keen eye on human behavior, and then dip it all in a big vat of Brooklyn getouttaheah humor. You don't get combo platters like that.[2]

Former San Francisco 49ers quarterback Steve Young described Cohn this way:

"Lowell Cohn was tough, absolutely brutal sometimes. He was like the power-washer blasting the barnacles off the boat—a steel-wool scouring pad extricating any and all blemishes from the pan, no matter how ingrained they might be. Simply put, you did not want to be the subject of one of Lowell's columns, but you always read them."[3]

Cohn said of himself, "Readers hated me, but they read me. Made assumptions about what I was like without ever meeting me."[4]

Before interviewing Cohn for this book in May 2023, this author made assumptions. I thought Cohn would be bristly, defensive, possibly even antagonistic when discussing his coverage of the born-again Giants. On the contrary, I found him gracious, patient, honest, and encouraging. It was the best interview I ever experienced.

Did Cohn just mellow with age? He acknowledged in the interview that may have been the case. But those positive qualities did not appear out of thin air. They are part of him.

Cohn spoke openly about his religious background:

I grew up in Brooklyn, New York, in the Flatbush Jewish ghetto. And my whole life has been informed by that. When I was a kid, I was in an Orthodox synagogue, and I was bar mitzvah of course at thirteen. I am a fervent Jew. I feel that everything about me is informed by my Judaism—how I think, how I look, how I sound, how I write. Judaism is a very complex religion. And part of it is, it's very conservative. Because we honor the past, our traditions, Abraham, Isaac and Jacob, Moses, David, all of that. My temperament is very much like that.

Now of course Jews are also social reformers. I'm not talking about that aspect of it. I'm talking about tradition. And I am bound to the tradition. I read about Judaism all the time, I read from the Bible.

I did marry a non-Jewish woman. She was brought up a Catholic. But she wasn't a Catholic. She never converted [to Judaism], but we did have a Jewish home. Our son, who is now thirty-five, had a bar mitzvah. And it was her idea. She said, when he was about eight, "When are we going to send him to Hebrew School?" I don't particularly go to synagogue, although I just bought a new yarmulke on Amazon, and I think I'm going to go this Friday night.

My wife died fifteen months ago and it's made me, I'm not going to say, spiritual, but searching. I think a lot about heaven. Now I was never taught about heaven. My Catholic friends say it was central to what they would talk about in church. In my Hebrew school and my synagogue, I never even heard the word. But now I hope that there is a heaven so I can meet my wife again. My older son says, "You're such a Jew, but you want to believe in the Christian idea of heaven." And my attitude is "Yeah! I want to meet Mom again."[5]

A conversation Cohn still remembers clearly, one he had with Johnnie LeMaster, illustrates the chasm between the beliefs of this Brooklyn Jew and those of the born-again Giants. A native of Paintsville, Kentucky, population about 6,500, LeMaster returned there after he retired from baseball. He serves as an elder at the Paintsville Church of Christ, has gone on mission trips to Peru, Panama, India, and Africa, and hosts a Facebook podcast called "A Short Stop with a Shortstop" in which he draws parallels between baseball and the Christian faith.

Cohn related:

LeMaster, again, I cannot tell you how lovely he is. I'm wild about Johnnie. And he was curious about me. Johnnie's from Kentucky. And I'm a Brooklyn Jew. And he didn't know, he had no experience of a person like me. So one day, before a game, we were just chatting, maybe by the batting cage, and because he was curious and really a gentleman, he said, "What religion are you?" Because he wanted to know. And I said, "Can you take a guess?" And he said, "Catholic."

Now, anybody who's really worldly would never think I'm a Catholic guy. I mean, I've got the tribal honker, everything. Now I realized he didn't even know what a Jew was. He thought the world was either Protestants or Catholics.

And I said, "Johnnie, I'm Jewish and I'm from New York." And he didn't disapprove. He gave a look of wanting to understand, because in his world, I was probably like a Zoroastrian to him. So I remember that. I'll never forget that. It's maybe 40 years ago, and I thought, He's trying hard to understand me. Now he has to rethink this. And I thought again, This is because he's such a lovely person.[6]

Cohn admitted that the beliefs of the born-again ballplayers baffled him. He said:

Yes, it seemed strange to me. Again, I didn't disapprove. But it was as foreign to me as I was to Johnnie. I mean, I had come from a Jewish ghetto. So this stuff, all these things that people would talk about, "Jesus is in my life," or "Jesus is my friend," or "I have to thank Jesus or God for this win or for my athletic ability," it was another language to me. I had no lens, no receptors, to understand it. I didn't disapprove of it, but I had to learn, I had to understand, because I had no idea where they were coming from.[7]

Apart from the three satirical pieces discussed in the previous chapter, a serious column he wrote about Dave Dravecky in 1989, and a satirical piece he wrote about Brett Butler in 1990, Cohn seldom wrote about the beliefs of the born-again ballplayers.

"They never ever discussed religion with me except when Johnnie asked about the satire and asked if I was Catholic," said Cohn. "Plus, I would never ask about it. It would not be relevant to the kinds of questions I was asking."[8]

He did write about a conversation he had with Mickey Marvin of the Oakland Raiders in 1983:

Mickey Marvin came over. "Don't leave without visiting," he said. I went back to his locker. We made small talk for a while, and then the conversation shifted to religion. It always does with Mickey. He is a fundamentalist Christian and he sees every particle of life through the filter of his beliefs. With some guys, I find that oppressive. With him, I don't.

"Do you believe in the devil?" I asked.

His face grew red and he leaned back in awe. "I take the devil very seriously," he whispered. "I believe in the devil as surely as I believe there's a heaven and a hell. The devil is very powerful. Make no mistake about that. But the Lord is more powerful." A glow passed over Mickey's face as he contemplated the Lord's omnipotence.[9]

Reminded of this interview, Cohn said, "I said in the quote that I found it oppressive. In retrospect, they [Christian athletes, including the God Squadders] didn't bother me with it, so maybe I was overstating the case."[10]

He did, however, give an example of a Christian athlete whose responses in interviews he did find obnoxious:

> *Let me be clear, because I'm trying to be as honest as possible. Probably I knew more about the God Squad-ism from the general talk about it than from the players themselves. I don't remember Jack Clark, maybe Lavelle, but I don't remember a specific incident, or Knepper, ever really saying things like that to me [espousing their Christian beliefs].*
>
> *I'll give you an example. In football, Kurt Warner was a great quarterback. And I think he was with St. Louis at the time and they were in the Super Bowl. And it used to be, I don't cover it anymore, there would be like a week of interviews before the game. It was a big deal.*
>
> *And every time you would talk to Kurt Warner, you would ask him anything, and he would talk about Jesus and God. And after a while, that I found oppressive. It really pissed me off because first of all, he wasn't answering any questions. We were trying to talk about football, and he was doing that all the time. In addition, he said the same things all the time. So I wasn't getting any particular insight into God or his feelings about God. It was hard for a journalist. That I found oppressive.*
>
> *I notice now that he's an announcer, he doesn't do that at all. Because I think they would kick him off because viewers would find him repetitive and narrow minded. I'm not questioning his faith, by the way. He's entitled to it. But to rub it in my face all the time was hard. I never had that experience at the Giants.*[11]

How did Cohn feel about Glenn Dickey's column urging the Giants to "trade one or two of the born-agains on that club, to break up that clique," and stating that "at the very least their lockers should be separated in the clubhouse?" Cohn told this author:

> *I disagree. First of all, there probably was a clique. You're allowed to be with your friends, you know what I mean? You're allowed to have lockers near your friends and you're allowed to socialize with your friends.*
>
> *In addition, I don't agree with Vida [Blue]. I think those guys were kickass competitors. I loved Vida and I'm so sorry he's gone. It hurt me when Vida died. But I think they were competitors.*
>
> *Also, I think Frank Robinson [Giants manager from 1981 to 1984] may have agreed with Vida. Frank was a very sarcastic and sometimes harsh kind of guy. I had a feeling he agreed with Vida. But I don't agree with Frank on that. So I don't think any of them should have been traded unless they weren't good players or they could get a good deal for them. But not on the basis of their religious beliefs.* [12]

In that same column, Dickey wrote, "Prayer meetings should be held outside the clubhouse." Cohn responded:

> *I have a feeling about that. First of all, I'm not sure they do or ever did pray in the clubhouse. I never saw it. They used to have Sunday chapel. But I don't think it was in the clubhouse.*
>
> *And I think two things. One, you're allowed to have Sunday chapel. And if the Jews want to have a Saturday minyan [a quorum of ten men—or in some synagogues, men and women—over the age of thirteen required for traditional Jewish public worship], they can have that too.*

> *Whenever you want. But I don't think it should be in the clubhouse. I think there should be a separate room for it.*[13]

Lavelle confirmed to this author that the Giants' Baseball Chapel services were always held in a separate room, never in the clubhouse.[14]

Cohn continued:

> *I'm going to give you a little background on that. I covered the Niners a lot. I wrote a book on Bill Walsh. And I know that Bill, before every season, would get the team together, and he would say, "We're a football outfit. No one espouses political opinions in this locker room. And no one goes on a religious crusade. And if you do, I'll send you off to Buffalo. We talk about football in here."*
>
> *And that's what I feel about the Giants. And that's what I thought they did. They talked about baseball. But when they wanted to pray, they went into a separate room. Maybe Glenn knew something that I didn't know. I never saw them praying or kneeling in the clubhouse. And I've been in there thousands of times.*[15]

Cohn said he never discussed the God Squad with Dickey.

"Glenn and I are both very independent, so we wouldn't have talked about that," said Cohn. "Plus, I didn't want him, nor did he want me, to think I was questioning his ideas."[16]

Reflecting on his columns about the God Squadders, Cohn said:

> *I'm an old man. I hope I wasn't unfair to them. I think writing a satire is good fun. I didn't realize that Johnnie would*

take it literally because I didn't mean it literally. And God knows, I probably wrote 8,000 columns. I hope I didn't go after any of the so-called "God Squad" guys because they were God Squadders. I know I once wrote a very critical column of Jack Clark because I thought he was dogging it in the outfield, and I was critical of him. But I never was critical of him for being a God Squadder or a Christian.[17]

Notes

[1] Lowell Cohn, *Gloves Off: 40 Years of Unfiltered Sportswriting* (Petaluma, CA: Roundtree Press, 2020), 13.

[2] Lowell Cohn, *Gloves Off: 40 Years of Unfiltered Sportswriting* (Petaluma, CA: Roundtree Press, 2020), 10.

[3] Lowell Cohn, *Gloves Off: 40 Years of Unfiltered Sportswriting* (Petaluma, CA: Roundtree Press, 2020), 8.

[4] Lowell Cohn, *Gloves Off: 40 Years of Unfiltered Sportswriting* (Petaluma, CA: Roundtree Press, 2020), 13.

[5] Lowell Cohn, interview with author, May 23, 2023.

[6] Lowell Cohn, interview with author, May 23, 2023.

[7] Lowell Cohn, interview with author, May 23, 2023.

[8] Lowell Cohn, interview with author, May 23, 2023.

[9] Lowell Cohn, "The Good Guys," *San Francisco Chronicle*, January 21, 1983, 65.

[10] Lowell Cohn, interview with author, May 23, 2023.

[11] Lowell Cohn, interview with author, May 23, 2023.

[12] Lowell Cohn, interview with author, May 23, 2023.

[13] Lowell Cohn, interview with author, May 23, 2023.

[14] Gary Lavelle, interview with author, June 1, 2023.

[15] Lowell Cohn, interview with author, May 23, 2023.

[16] Lowell Cohn, interview with author, May 23, 2023.

[17] Lowell Cohn, interview with author, May 23, 2023.

Chapter 15
Scapegoats

An *Examiner* feature story in May 1981 written by Giants fan John Kerner Jr. about his experience watching the team in spring training gave a glimpse into God Squad scapegoating:

> *Sitting behind us in the stands during one of the games were some friends and fans of Giants pitcher Tom Griffin. They asked me why the Bay Area press were so focused on the negative aspects of the "religious" players on the team, the so-called "God squad." My reply was that I felt the press needed a scapegoat to explain mediocre play. Other teams have religious players and frequent prayer meetings but no one seems to criticize them.*[1]

As Art Spander wrote in the *Examiner* in 1981, "A couple of years ago some people would not condone the way the Giants played, San Francisco falling apart in the 1979 season after contending for the championship much of 1978. Seeking answers, some sports writers were quick to blame the growing membership of 'born-again' Christians."[2]

In June 1981, Gary Lavelle told Noma Faingold of the *California Aggie*, "I feel the papers, specifically in the Bay Area, have probably distorted many of the players' beliefs, therefore probably causing the controversy that exists right now."

Speaking about 1978, Lavelle added, "We were doing

very well. A lot of the guys who were Christians were just praising the Lord for the ability He'd given them to play the game of baseball. Reporters, more or less, interpreted that as if we were thanking the Lord for giving us a good game. The players were not doing that. We were just thanking the Lord for the ability to play the game."

Talking about 1979, Lavelle continued, "When things started going bad, reporters were saying, 'Well, where's your faith now?' The faith was still there, but because we weren't doing well, they [reporters] thought we were backing off from our beliefs, that we were making God great when things were going good, then we were forgetting him when things were going bad. It was really distorted."

He added, "When you're having a bad year, such as the Giants were having last year [1980], you're always looking for scapegoats. People are going to pick at anything they feel could possibly explain the reason why you're losing or having difficulties and I think we were the scapegoats. They thought that because we had a good group of Christians, that possibly they were being pacified by their faith and not giving 100 percent."[3]

As Knepper described it, "It's really funny—in '78 when we all became Christians, it was really great, because we came out of nowhere to lead the division the entire year and we finished third. Then in '79 and '80 when the team didn't live up to expectations, it was blamed on the Christians. What became popular then suddenly became unpopular. We took a lot of heat."[4]

Talking about the Giants' slide from contenders in 1978 to a dismal 1979 season, Vida Blue threw some gas on the fire. Glenn Dickey wrote:

Blue thought part of the problem was religion in the clubhouse. It was an era when Born Again Christians were becoming very public in baseball, and nowhere more than in the Giants clubhouse.

"We always had our Sunday morning chapel," said Blue, "but now, some of these guys were wanting to have meetings during the week. I've got nothing against religion and I believe everybody has the right to worship whatever God he wants to in his house or in his church, but doing this in the clubhouse created cliques. You can't have one group of guys in one corner of the clubhouse and another group in another. It just doesn't work. It also got to the point where guys were saying it was God's will. If a pitcher lost a game, it was because that was what God wanted. If a hitter struck out with the bases loaded, same thing. That's bull. The pitcher didn't make his pitches, the batter couldn't hit that hard slider on the outside corner. You can't make excuses. You have to do the job."[5]

A May 1979 article by Peter Gammons of *The Boston Globe* explored the issue, getting feedback from Giants pitcher-player representative John Curtis and Bill Madlock:

"The feeling is that most of the writers are brutally negative," says Curtis, "And I don't mean in the conventional sense, because I realize players often don't realize what the role of the media is supposed to be. But there's a feeling that the people writing out here don't care and don't know what they're talking about, they just rip."

... As Curtis and others point out, much of the coverage—particularly in the Chronicle—is scapegoat journalism.

> "It's always negative," says Bill Madlock. "Something always has to be someone's fault, If the pitchers are in a slump, it's the pitching coach. Lose a game, it's the manager's fault. Look at this year. The manager of the year [Altobelli] in 1978 they want fired one month into 1979. Same with the executive of the year [Spec Richardson]. Same with the players. We lost two out of three to the Dodgers [April 20–22] and they buried us. 'No chance.' Then we lost eight in a row on the road and we were the worst team in baseball."[6]

Gammons was not all that sympathetic, adding, "In the media's defense, these are not the A's. The Giants are an excuse-making team that can run off under the shelter of the Lord when they lose."[7]

At least one non-God Squadder got tired of the writers harping on this theme.

"A lot of times the ballgame seems to be a footnote to what has been said," Darrell Evans noted in 1981. "That kind of stuff overshadows the game. Like right now, we have the God Squad articles. What's the big deal? What's that got to do with anything? That's what bothers me."[8]

Knepper said, " . . . the Bay Area social climate is not supportive of the Christian lifestyle. So there are a lot of unhappy things to write about. But there is no reason for a writer to write garbage, just to sell papers . . . and then other players read that garbage and know it's not the truth, and wonder how they can write stuff like that."[9]

San Jose Mercury columnist Dan Hruby defended the born-again Giants in 1981:

> *I'm inclined to agree with Houston pitcher Bob Knepper*

when he says blaming the Giants' problems last year on the so-called "God Squad" was off base. Knepper, after losing a game, supposedly told manager Dave Bristol he wasn't upset because it was God's will.

Knepper, traded by San Francisco after last season, says "The story isn't true." And he adds, "The Bay Area media jumped on the Giants who professed to be Christians. Nothing was said about Oakland, which has far more Christians." Indeed, the A's may have more. Their leader is Wayne Gross, who says between 15 and 18 teammates regularly attend Sunday chapel services. Maybe the A's have been more subtle about their religious preferences.[10]

Hall of Fame pitcher Don Sutton commented:

One of the things I've found disconcerting through the years is that people in (the media) go out of their way to highlight and write up and rip people who are spiritually minded. In contrast, those same people will go out of their way to sweep under the rug all of those guys who want to be out all night. It's like, "The players looking for hookers and booze, let's protect them. But let's massacre the guys who are spiritually minded." I don't get it.[11]

In a preview of the 1980 season, Bruce Jenkins of the *Chronicle* wrote of the Giants, "It will help, too, if the players stick to the business of baseball. The presence of manager Dave Bristol should eliminate the petty bickering, and a downplay of the 'born-again' religious atmosphere would help, too. This club has talent, but it's time to start showing it."[12]

Sportswriters across the nation, who for the most part

never spoke directly with the born-again Giants, picked up on this theme. Gammons, in a preview of the 1980 season, wrote of the Giants, "First priority is to get rid of God Squad clique, which means Knepper, reliever Gary Lavelle and possibly even Jack Clark could go."[13] Had Gammons been reading too much Glenn Dickey?

Gammons was hammering the same theme that winter, writing about the trade talks, "The Giants are going to trade pitching and break up its God Squad: Gary Lavelle, Bob Knepper and John Montefusco are all available, as is first baseman Mike Ivie."[14] Gammons didn't do his homework. Montefusco was never part of the God Squad.

Gammons kept beating the same drum when Frank Robinson was hired to manage the Giants in February 1981:

So that he might be fully prepared for his new job as manager of the Giants, friends have given Frank Robinson a few suggestions. Go to theological school, so he can understand the infamous God Squad, not to mention what's in the display rack of books in the locker of relief pitcher Gary Lavelle . . .

He has been briefed on the background of the God Squad, which in essence is what got Dave Bristol fired in the middle of last December's winter meetings. He has heard the stories of how the departed Bob Knepper told Bristol on the mound not to blame him for a gopher ball, but that it was God's will. And how loss after loss was explained away as divine justice. And how it all caved in on slugging first baseman Mike Ivie, causing him to quit and causing Bristol to call him a "cancer."[15]

In one paragraph, Gammons succeeded in perpetuating

or creating four myths: the Knepper "God's will" legend, born-again Christians accepting losing as divine justice, Ivie quitting because of the born-again controversy, and, last but not least, that the God Squad was responsible for Bristol being fired.

It was one thing for the press to blame the God Squadders for losses. But it was unconscionable to pin Bristol's dismissal on the born-again players.

Dick Young, who wrote a nationally-syndicated column for the *New York Daily News*, got that ball rolling. When Giants owner Bob Lurie fired Bristol in December 1980, Young wrote, "There is a scary undertone to this story. It is something that people in the business are just starting to talk about, in half-hushed voices. It involves religion, and people are very careful how they talk about religious things, and write about them."[16]

Young should have taken his own advice, because he went on to make these unfounded statements:

> *They tell of a player, a pitcher, who had two strikes on a batter, made a bad pitch, and had it hit out of the ballpark. The manager went to the mound to ask what the hell was going on.*
>
> *"It was God's will," said the pitcher.*
>
> *The feeling of predestination is growing among the God Squadders. It presents a distinct problem to managers. It can test a manager's patience. It did Dave Bristol's. It is believed to have been a major factor in his dismissal, creating a schism between him and his club owner, Bob Lurie . . . It is a strange development, and there will be repercussions, but the feeling is strong that Dave Bristol was shot down by the God Squad that he dared contest.*[17]

There is zero evidence that Lurie fired Bristol because of the faith of Mike Ivie or his born-again Christian teammates. Lurie took issue with Bristol telling Glenn Dickey in October 1980, "We've got to get rid of the cancer on this club," a reference which included Ivie. Lurie's problem was that Bristol went public with the criticism. In Dickey's column, Bristol never said the issue was with Ivie's born-again faith. Instead, Bristol pointed to Ivie's penchant for retiring and then un-retiring and for the first baseman leaving the team before the end of the season because of a back ailment instead of supporting the club from the bench.

When Lurie pulled the plug on Bristol in December 1980, he explained his decision this way: "It was just a variety of things—different opinions, how things should be handled."[18]

Bristol told the *Chronicle*, "I'm sure the Dickey column had something to do with it, and that's nobody's fault but mine."[19]

So neither Lurie nor Bristol blamed the born-again beliefs of Ivie or his Christian teammates for the firing. Bristol took full responsibility. That didn't stop other sportswriters from running with Dick Young's unsupported accusation, which he repeated in January 1981 when Frank Robinson was hired to replace Bristol.

"The so-called God-squad, a group of born-again, losing-is-predestined mentalities, had much to do with the undermining of Robby's predecessor [Bristol]," wrote Young. "I expect Frank Robby will read them some facts of life, and it won't be from the New Testament."[20]

Dave Jones repeated the allegation in the *Chicago Tribune*, where he wrote, "Bristol, also a religious man, reportedly could not accept that when a man failed to perform on the field it was 'God's will.' When he voiced his opinion that he thought that kind of determination was having a negative influence, he was out."[21]

F.M. Williams wrote in *The Tennessean*, "Bristol ran afoul of the group [the God Squad] last summer when he called Mike Ivie, a member of the Giants' religious group, a cancer on the ballclub . . . The movement becomes a problem when it affects motivation."[22]

In *The Sacramento Bee*, Bill Conlin declared, "Few will doubt there were instances last season with Dave Bristol at the Giants' helm that the inmates were running the asylum. Bristol, too, was supposed to be a firm and resolute manager, and perhaps he was. But Bristol had to deal with too many flakes, including, if you'll pardon seeming irreverence, the God Squad."[23]

In the Binghamton (New York) *Press and Sun Bulletin*, Russ Worman wrote, "It's up to Frank Robinson to restore semblance of baseball order at Candlestick Park. The Giants' God Squad got the last manager, Dave Bristol, on the grounds of 'philosophical differences' and failure to communicate."[24]

Some sportswriters also blamed the God Squad for Joe Altobelli being fired in early September 1979. Ken Nigro of *The Baltimore Sun* wrote in 1982, "Altobelli was hired to pilot San Francisco and was named manager of the year in 1978 for guiding the Giants to an 89–73 record. Altobelli was dismissed near the end of the following season, however, when he couldn't control several members of the so-called Giants 'God Squad.' "[25]

In a preview of the 1980 Giants, Ken Leiker of *The Arizona Republic* chimed in, stating, "Altobelli also had to contend with a born-again religious cult, whose disciples used their new-found Christianity as an excuse."[26]

When the Orioles tabbed Altobelli in November 1982 to manage the team in 1983, Jim Henneman of the *Baltimore Evening Sun* wrote:

> . . . *Altobelli managed the San Francisco Giants for three years, earning National League "Manager of the Year" honors in 1978, and then being fired the next year with 20 games remaining in the season. He got mixed reviews during his tenure with the Giants, mainly because he apparently was unable to control a clubhouse that bordered on the violent at times.*
>
> *"On balance, taking everything into consideration, he was a good manager," said one West Coast observer who followed Altobelli throughout his stint in San Francisco. "They made a good run of it in 1978 [when the Giants finished third, 89–73], but it all fell apart the next year."*
>
> *That was when the Giants split into factions, with a large group of born-again Christians, dubbed the "God Squad," apparently split from the rest of the team.*[27]

That unproven assertion had a long shelf life. In October 1983, after Altobelli had led the Orioles to a World Series championship, Steve Jacobson wrote in *Newsday*:

> *In his second year in San Francisco, the Giants won 89 games, their most in eight seasons, and he [Altobelli] was named the National League Manager of the Year. Left-handers Vida Blue and Bob Knepper were big winners. The next season the team came apart in his hands, split into factions and cliques, at the center of which was that unit known as the "God Squad."*[28]

But in 1983 Altobelli told Alan Goldstein of *The Sun*, "I know a lot of guys felt I was a victim of the 'God Squad.' A pitcher would throw a gopher ball and say, 'it was God's will,' but I don't get caught up in all of that. I don't think the man upstairs is going to do me any special favors. The guy across the field can pray just as hard."[29]

So Altobelli denied that the God Squad was the cause of his dismissal, but at the same time perpetuated the "God's will" myth.

Examiner columnist Art Spander, who was the only Bay Area sportswriter in Cincinnati the day Altobelli was fired after a loss to the Reds on September 5, 1979, could only speculate as to why the manager was canned, writing:

> *How did the dreams of spring evolve into the nightmare of Indian summer? Why are the Giants, who are planning a pennant, now just hoping to survive? Is it because the locker room is rife with evangelists? Or because [General Manager Spec] Richardson doesn't know a ballplayer from a bowler? Or because the clubhouse occasionally reminded you of a student demonstration in Berkeley? Or because the pitching staff made the home run de rigeur? Or because [Owner Bob] Lurie took a week's vacation in Maui? Maybe it was all those things, but obviously Lurie and Richardson believed it was because Altobelli didn't get what he should out of his athletes.*[30]

None of the subsequent articles on Altobelli's firing in the *Examiner* and *Chronicle*, written by local reporters, the ones closest to the inner workings of the Giants, made any mention of the God Squad being the cause. Glenn Schwarz of the *Examiner* pinpointed the problem on Altobelli isolating himself from the players, leading to a lack of communication and rapport.³¹

Lurie, who fired Altobelli, never alluded to the God Squad as a reason. He pointed to the Giants' poor record, 61–79, including a 4–18 mark in the last three weeks before Altobelli's dismissal.

But, as with Bristol's firing, too many sportswriters were not about to let the truth get in the way of a sensational story. Once a writer published an unconfirmed rumor, other writers used that as source material to spread the misinformation like wildfire. They were either too slothful to check the veracity of the accounts or too happy to disseminate stories that might sell newspapers.

Knepper spoke with this author about his relationship with the San Francisco sportswriters:

As far as I know, I was never interviewed by Glenn [Dickey] or Lowell [Cohn], which was one of the sad points about them. They never interviewed any of us Christians that I was ever aware of. In fact, I bet I never actually saw them in the locker room except for Glenn walking straight through the locker room on his way to the dugout, never stopping to say a word to anybody.¹

I did have one confrontation of sorts with a writer during my second stint with the Giants [1989–90]. I think his name was Dave and he wrote for a paper down on the peninsula [south of San Francisco]. But it really wasn't much of a confrontation, as he literally ran away from me in the locker room. Was pretty sad to see such cowardice.

---

[1] Bob Knepper, interview with author, June 17, 2023. Lowell Cohn responded in an interview with the author on June 18, 2023: "I didn't know Knepper well. Maybe I never interviewed him. He may be correct. But I certainly knew LeMaster and Lavelle. And I was in the clubhouse often."

I think what hurt so much was being blindsided by the writers when I assumed we were all getting along fine. I was very naive and too trusting with sportswriters when I first got to the big leagues, and I paid the price.[32]

Notes

[1] Dr. John Kerner Jr., "Love, Marriage and the Giants," *San Francisco Examiner*, May 10, 1981, 294.

[2] Art Spander, "The Giants, God and Satan," *San Francisco Examiner*, May 12, 1981, 51.

[3] Noma Faingold, "Lavelle Answers Critics of 'God Squad,' " *California Aggie*, June 9, 1981, 4.

[4] Larry Stone, "Ten Years Later, God Squad Makes Comeback," *Santa Rosa Press Democrat*, September 24, 1989, C-3.

[5] Glenn Dickey, *San Francisco Giants 40 Years* (San Francisco: Woodford Press, 1997), 100.

[6] Peter Gammons, "Bad Vibes By the Bay," *The Boston Globe*, May 18, 1979, 76.

[7] Peter Gammons, "Bad Vibes By the Bay," *The Boston Globe*, May 18, 1979, 76.

[8] Bob Padecky, "Players' View of the Press," *The Sacramento Bee*, May 16, 1981, 62.

[9] Stan Hochman, "Knepper Thankful Home is Dome," *Philadelphia Daily News*, October 9, 1981, 122.

[10] Dan Hruby, "Krafcisin, Lingenfelter Possible Warrior Picks," *San Jose Mercury*, June 6, 1981, 93.

[11] Terence Moore, "The God Squad: Many Pros Keep Faith in Play All Week," *Atlanta Journal-Constitution*, August 5, 2001, A-1.

[12] Bruce Jenkins, "Dodgers Picked 1st—Giants 4th," *San Francisco Chronicle*, April 10, 1980, 64.

[13] Peter Gammons, "A Look at the Trade Mart," *The Boston Globe*, October 19, 1980, 49.

[14] Peter Gammons, "Will Baseball Talks Be Trade Bonanza or Bust?" *The Boston Globe*, published in the *Atlanta Journal-Constitution*, December 5, 1980, 63.

[15] Peter Gammons, "Franks' Back," *The Boston Globe*, February 17, 1981, 29.

[16] Dick Young, "Bristol Didn't Have a Prayer with 'God Squad,'" *New York Daily News*, December 11, 1980, C-24.

[17] Dick Young, "Bristol Didn't Have a Prayer with 'God Squad,'" *New York Daily News*, December 11, 1980, C-24.

[18] Ira Miller, "Why Was Bristol Fired? Only Bob Lurie Knows," *San Francisco Chronicle*, December 10, 1980, 69.

[19] Ira Miller, "Why Was Bristol Fired? Only Bob Lurie Knows," *San Francisco Chronicle*, December 10, 1980, 73.

[20] Dick Young, "Celebrity Status Dulls Cooney's Training," *New York Daily News*, January 17, 1981, 167.

[21] Dave Jones, "Sports Briefing: A Giant Problem," *Chicago Tribune*, December 14, 1980, section 4, 5.

[22] F. M. Williams, "Sports Scope: The Grab Bag," *The Tennessean*, December 17, 1980, 31.

[23] Bill Conlin, "Robbie and Racism," *The Sacramento Bee*, January 20, 1981, 32.

[24] Russ Worman, "National League Preview," *Binghamton Press and Sun Bulletin*, April 5, 1981, 21.

[25] Ken Nigro, "O's Interview Altobelli for Manager Job," *The Baltimore Sun*, October 10, 1982, 22.

[26] Ken Leiker, "Giants," *The Arizona Republic*, February 10, 1980, 31.

[27] Jim Henneman, "Joe Altobelli Won't Break Birds' Stride," *The Evening Sun*, November 12, 1982, 41.

[28] Steve Jacobson, "A Long Wait for the Champagne," *Newsday*, October 18, 1983, 98.

[29] Alan Goldstein, "Altobelli Paid his Dues in Bushes and at 'Frisco,'" *The Baltimore Sun*, October 10, 1983, 25.

[30] Art Spander, "Why the Ax Fell on Altobelli," *San Francisco Examiner*, September 6, 1978, 65.

[31] Glenn Schwarz, "Altobelli Always Did Like Rochester," *San Francisco Examiner*, September 7, 1979, 56.

[32] Bob Knepper, interview with author, June 17, 2023.

Chapter 16
Baseball Chapel

As Terence Moore wrote in the *Atlanta Journal-Constitution*, "Most staunchly religious players in baseball remained in hiding after the turn of the century through the 1960s. Don Kessinger and Randy Hundley of the Chicago Cubs were among the exceptions. They led informal services for teammates in their hotel rooms on road trips. Harmon Killebrew and Al Worthington did the same for the Twins."[1]

In the early 1960s, Bobby Richardson, Tony Kubek, and announcer Red Barber held Sunday devotionals for the New York Yankees. They and a few other players met for about twenty minutes in a hotel or banquet room to pray, hear a brief Bible message, and discuss the message. Sometime in the 1960s, they changed the venue to a weight room or other facility at the ballpark itself. As late as 1972, the Twins and Cubs were still the only teams holding Sunday religious services for their teams on road trips.

In 1973 Warren Spoelstra, Detroit sportswriter and former president of the Baseball Writers Association of America, approached Commissioner of Baseball Bowie Kuhn with the idea of creating a chapel program for every major league team. Spoelstra explained to Kuhn the problem Christian ballplayers had getting to church when their team had an early Sunday afternoon ballgame. Kuhn approved and the non-denominational organization Baseball Chapel was born in 1973.

During its first year, twelve teams participated in Baseball Chapel. By 1975 every major league team had a Sunday chapel service and in 1978 chapel expanded to the minor leagues and winter ball in Latin America. In 1982 Spoelstra turned over the leadership of Baseball Chapel to Bobby Richardson,

Lloyd Mashore, who became senior pastor at Concord (California) Christian Center in 1973, was a spiritual mentor to the God Squad. He was just a baseball fan who regularly brought his three sons to games at Candlestick Park. Someone introduced him to Gary Lavelle, who invited Mashore to his home in Foster City to lead Bible studies for the born-again Giants when they were playing at home. Sometimes the sessions were held in the home of the Mashores or the Kneppers. William Endicott of the *Los Angeles Times* described one meeting held in 1979:

> *The six of them, all major league baseball players with the San Francisco Giants, sat with their wives or girlfriends in the den of pitcher Bob Knepper's new suburban home, praying, singing hymns to the accompaniment of a guitar and reading the Bible.*
>
> *. . . Relief pitcher Tom Griffin offered a personal testimony. "There was a time," he said, "when success was really all I cared about and the money I would be making. Highs and lows were really extreme. But that was before Christ entered my life. Since I accepted the Lord, things have really leveled off."*
>
> *Catcher Marc Hill, on the disabled list with a broken wrist, wondered if "the Lord is testing me," and utility infielder Rob Andrews, who is having a frustrating season and rarely is in the starting lineup, said that "if the Lord*

decides to take me from this situation and put me in a starting position, I'll be ready."[2]

Mashore's involvement with the home Bible studies evolved into his bringing in speakers for the Giants' Sunday chapel services.

Back then, said Mashore, the speakers were not necessarily Christians and gave motivational talks to help players' performance. It was only later that the Giants Sunday chapel speakers were born-again believers giving a Christian message, so that the event was more like church.[3]

"Usually we would have eight to ten guys," recalled Lavelle, who served both as the Giants' player representative and the team's representative for Baseball Chapel. "A lot of guys would come in and listen to what the speaker had to say. We set it up for the visiting team [also], but usually the chapels were done separately."[4]

Mashore got to know some of the God Squadders intimately.

"At that time, Rob Andrews was going through some personal identity questions about his own faith," said Mashore, "and so Rob ended up staying with us on the homestands. He stayed with us in our home and was in charge of one of our bedrooms. Very, very personable. Rob was still new in his faith and he ended up attending our church there in Concord and ultimately met his wife there, and a few years later they were married and began to build their life together."[5]

Mashore married them. He also baptized Jack Clark in the Mashores' backyard swimming pool in July 1978.

Mashore helped Mike Ivie navigate his emotional turmoil as a Giant.

"I had a real close working relationship with Mike Ivie," said Mashore, "and traveled to Georgia with him to meet his family and to kind of let them know how we were encouraging Mike in his Christian faith. And they were very interested in supporting and encouraging us inasmuch as we were working with their son."[6]

Mashore met with Ivie often, including when Ivie retired and then returned to the Giants a few weeks later in the summer of 1980.

"There were times when I met with Mike to encourage him and to be a friend who wasn't judging him for his batting average or his next contract or any of that that weighed on his mind a lot," said Mashore. "I was there to just be a friend."[7]

He maintained a close relationship with Lavelle while Gary was a Giant. He is still in touch with Knepper, who Mashore said had "an appetite for knowledge."

Surprisingly, he said one topic that never came up in his individual interactions with the God Squadders was the negative reaction of the press to their professions of faith.

"I know there was kind of an adversarial relationship with some of the press or some of the major league machine," he said, "but it was something that wasn't really front and center to any of our conversations."[8]

He was aware of the uproar over Knepper's supposed "God's will" statement.

Mashore remarked, "That particular incident, I don't have any documents, but I believe that was a sportswriter of some sort that did an interview with Bob and I think the common knowledge was that it was a misquote."[9]

Some God-Squadders were more regular in chapel attendance than others, said Mashore, preferring to devote more time to on-field preparation..

Writing for the *Examiner* on July 12, 1978, Jim Vaszko noted that sixteen Giants players and two coaches attended a Sunday chapel at Candlestick before the final game of a four-game series against the Cincinnati Reds. Vaszko listed some in attendance. In addition to Lavelle, LeMaster, Clark, Knepper, Andrews, Whitfield, Madlock, Herndon, and Moffitt—Willie McCovey and Darrell Evans, two key cogs in the Giants' offense—were on hand.

Several of those in attendance would not have identified themselves as born-again Christians.

As Gary Swan of the *Chronicle* noted, "As in all congregations, there are varying degrees of religiousness among ballplayers. There are zealots—evangelical, born-again Christians. There are lukewarm believers—occasional churchgoers during the offseason. Then there are those who, according to longtime Tigers announcer and occasional preacher Ernie Harwell, 'just happen to wander in to see what's going on.' "[10]

Vaszko humorously noted, "Only eight Reds were in attendance, a crucial fact I thought might bode well for the Giants' chances in the game that was to be played later in the day. I was sorely mistaken as the Giants were drubbed 8–2."[11]

Among the Reds attending were George Foster, who served as the team's chapel leader, Ken Griffey, and Dave Concepcion.

The Giants were leading the division when Vaszko published his column. Tongue in cheek, he wondered whether God was on the Giants' side because of their abundance of believers. He wrote, "Personally, I don't care where the Giants finish this year. But I'm more than willing to confess the error of my ways should current circumstances persist through, oh, say, the beginning of October."[12]

Although Vaszko probably was just being funny, he may have summarized the cultural notion of how born-again Christians think God works with wins and losses on a baseball team.

Should born-again Christian ballplayers pray for victory?

Rigo Lopez, Spanish Chaplain to the Giants, also serves as Metro Director in the San Francisco Bay Area for the Fellowship of Christian Athletes (FCA). This author attended, as a journalist, an FCA meeting, called a "huddle," that Lopez led for the Christian athletes at the University of San Francisco. It had been a frustrating beginning of the season for the Dons' baseball team, off to a sub-.500 start. As the huddle was closing, one of the baseball players asked the group to pray that the team would start winning.

Lopez asked the huddle members whether they thought God was concerned with wins and losses. He admitted that he had said prayers like that in his playing days (he had been a catcher for the Dons), but that his team often still lost. The huddle members agreed that God was more concerned with the attitude of the players, that they bond together and maintain unity. The player modified his prayer request.

In a similar vein, Dave Dravecky, born-again pitcher for the Giants in the late 1980s, recalled in a 2002 interview the teammate who occasionally attended chapel and "made you wonder, was he there because he wanted to be there? Or was he there because he went 0-for-4 and wanted to be 3-for-4?"[13]

Dravecky had made a more pointed comment in 1989.

"Christianity sadly has become a crutch," he said. "God's just some kind of trinket that you dangle out there just so you can go 4-for-4 in a game."[14]

In July 1980, the *Examiner* ran another piece about the Giants' God Squad. Terence Moore wrote:

> *It has been fashionable to label those with devote [sic] Christian beliefs in orange and black doubleknits as "God Squadders." And the eight or so diehards of the group don't shy away from their nickname, or their beliefs. They do feel, however, the attention has been slightly misplaced.*
>
> *"We used to have great turnouts to the chapel services and the Bible meetings that we have," said Bob Knepper. "But after all of the publicity, the attendance started tailing off. Some of the players were afraid to come because of what people might think."*[15]

Giants' bullpen coach John Van Ornum, who attended the chapel service that Moore covered, told him, "Why they put these ballplayers in a fishbowl just because they say they are Christians, I don't know. They don't make a big deal out of talking about engineers or doctors when they say they are Christians. I don't understand."[16]

Baseball Chapel generated some controversy.

Chapel services generally run fifteen to twenty minutes, but the Seattle Mariners ran afoul of management when some of their services went a bit too long. In the off-season after the 1986 campaign, Mariners' General Manager Dick Balderson said he was upset that the services sometimes ran overtime and caused those attending to be late for pre-game warmups. Assistant chapel leader Alvin Davis owned up to it.

"I agree with Dick that we did have some problems as far as being late," said Davis. "Whatever policy Dick sets, we're going to honor."[17]

Jim Reeves of the *Fort-Worth Star Telegram* wrote in February 1981:

> Critics of the movement also contend that it has split teams into factions and even led to the firing of Dave Bristol as manager of the San Francisco Giants at the winter meetings in December, an allegation Bristol publicly denies.
>
> Bristol also denies the story, circulating at the winter meetings, that a Giant pitcher, who gave up a home run after getting two strikes on a batter in a game last season, shrugged and said, "It was God's will," when Bristol came to the mound.
>
> "It [religion] never surfaced out in the clubhouse or on the field," Bristol declared from his home in North Carolina. "Other than Chapel on Sunday, it never came up. Nobody ever said anything to me about religion on that club, other than to ask if they could have Chapel."[18]

A week before the 1981 season began, the *New York Daily News* reported on new Giants manager's Frank Robinson relationship with the Giants' born-again players:

> Someone asked him [Robinson] . . . how he planned to handle the "God Squad." Those players whose religious fervor last year was considered detrimental to the ball club included pitcher Bob Knepper (since traded to Houston), pitcher Gary Lavelle and Ivie, and to a lesser degree, outfielder Jack Clark.
>
> "Yes, I heard about it," Robinson said. "But I haven't seen evidence of it since I came here, so I'm not concerned about it. There's no sense being concerned about something that happened last year."[19]

A few weeks into the 1981 season, Robinson still had no issues with the born-again players, as reported in *The Baltimore Sun*:

Last year, the word was out the Giants had taken this bornagain Christian thing too far, and that chapel had become more important than baseball.

"There's been no God Squad stuff this year," Robinson said. "It hasn't interfered with the play on the field. The players have their chapel services like other teams, but that's it. They've responded. They've already had a chance to bury their heads [because of the team's poor start to the season], but they've shown me they're willing."[20]

The bonds that the born-again Giants players formed through the chapel services and home Bible studies led to support for one another off the field. Lavelle, for example, was best man at Clark's wedding.

Some things did, indeed, become more important than baseball.

In 1979 Knepper's wife, Teri, gave birth three months prematurely to their son, Jacob. The boy was diagnosed with hyaline membrane disease, the same illness that killed President Kennedy's infant son.

For three days, Jacob hovered between life and death.

"I didn't know if I had a little baby or not," said Teri, twenty-three at the time. "It was very heart-breaking, it really hurt me to see him. You want to help so badly, but there's nothing you can do."[21]

One of the first things Bob did was call Mashore and Randy Helton, the pastor of the Kneppers' church. They in turn put Jacob on a "prayer chain," enlisting prayer for Jacob from the members of the church and other Christians. In addition, Bob, Helton, and Gary Lavelle went to Stanford Hospital the night Jacob was born and prayed for the child at 2 a.m.

Within a few days, Jacob, who had been on a respirator, was breathing on his own. Soon after, he was released from the hospital into the grateful arms of his parents, who could now enjoy their healthy, happy baby.

As Knepper explained in 1981 after being traded to the Astros, "It's not so much that baseball has lost importance to me, but my family and God have become more important. No matter how bad I do in baseball, I'll still have a family that loves me and a God that loves me. Now I can go out there and not worry about pitching bad."[22]

Dwight Chapin wrote in the *Examiner* about Dan Krainert, whose life was saved at age nineteen in 1980 via a heart transplant: "Special help also came from former Giants' pitcher Bob Knepper — 'He was the backbone of keeping me strong spiritually,' Krainert says — and other Giants such as Jack Clark and Gary Lavelle."[23]

The *Napa Valley Register* reported:

Knepper and Bobby Baker, considered the pastor of pro athletes in the Bay Area since he holds chapel services for the Giants, A's, 49ers and Raiders, spent a lot of time with Napa teen Dan Krainert before and after his heart transplant operation in December.

"I got more from Dan than I gave. He was a brave young man who showed a lot of courage to go through what he has," Knepper says.[24]

Notes

[1] Terence Moore, "Baseball and Religion," *Atlanta Journal-Constitution*, August 13,1989, C-1.

[2] William Endicott,. " 'Born Again' Ballplayers on Increase ," *Los Angeles Times*, August 31, 1979, 1.

[3] Lloyd Mashore, interview with author, May 20, 2023.

[4] Gary Lavelle, interview with author, June 1, 2023.

[5] Lloyd Mashore, interview with author, May 20, 2023.

[6] Lloyd Mashore, interview with author, May 20, 2023.

[7] Lloyd Mashore, interview with author, May 20, 2023.

[8] Lloyd Mashore, interview with author, May 20, 2023.

[9] Lloyd Mashore, interview with author, May 20, 2023.

[10] Gary Swan, "God and Baseball," *San Francisco Chronicle*, August 14, 1990, D-3.

[11] Jim Vaszko, "Baseball Players Do Think of Serious Things," *San Francisco Examiner*, July 12, 1978, 35.

[12] Jim Vaszko, "Baseball Players Do Think of Serious Things," *San Francisco Examiner*, July 12, 1978, 35.

[13] Richard Scheinin and Daniel Brown, "Sporting Their Faith: Heavenly Gestures by Bonds, Others Inspire Speculation," *San Jose Mercury News*, October 26, 2002, 1-E.

[14] Joan Connell, "The Hunger for Miracles," *The Mercury News*, August 19, 1989, 1E.

[15] Terence Moore, "The Giants' Bible Brigade," *San Francisco Examiner*, July 27, 1980, 31.

[16] Terence Moore, "The Giants' Bible Brigade," *San Francisco Examiner*, July 27, 1980, 31.

[17] Alvin Davis with Matt Sieger, "The Decision," *Venture*, May/June 1987, 5.

[18] Jim Reeves, "Dugout Religion," *Fort Worth Star Telegram*, February 8, 1981, 37.

[19] Norm Miller, "Robby Won't Be as Stern," *New York Daily News*, April 3, 1981, 258.

[20] Ken Nigro, "Robinson Calls Road Smoother on 2nd Chance," *The Baltimore Sun*, May 4, 1981, 38.

[21] Nancy Dooley, "Knepper Team's Rookie is Making It," *San Francisco Examiner*, July 1, 1979, 27.

[22] Stan Vaughn, "Faith Leads Knepper, Hubbard in Pro Sports Maze," *Napa Valley Register*, April 18, 1981, 8.

[23] Dwight Chapin, "A Matter of Heart," *San Francisco Examiner*, October 16, 1981, 39.

[24] Stan Vaughn, "Faith Leads Knepper, Hubbard in Pro Sports Maze," *Napa Valley Register*, April 18, 1981, 8.

Chapter 17
God Squad Sunset

By 1984, Glenn Dickey hadn't changed his tune. In a September 7 column he wrote:

The recent surge by the Giants may be the worst thing that could have happened to the club. Why? Because it will convince the front office—not the smartest in all of sports—that the club is really a good one, after all, and no major changes need be made. But if the Giants are ever to become serious contenders, they need to make a dramatic improvement in the infield defense, trade for at least one solid starter and—most important of all—break up the God Squad clique.[1]

On September 21 he wrote, "The Giants haven't had a leader since [Joe] Morgan left. They've got too many whiners and complainers and the 'Born Again' clique has too much power. [General Manager Tom] Haller knows who the bad apples are. He needs to clean them out."[2]

At least one *Chronicle* reader wasn't buying Dickey's solution. Lou Thomas wrote:

C.W. Nevius in his "What's Wrong with the Giants" article points to the Bob Knepper trade as a classic mistake. What he doesn't mention is that Glenn Dickey, your in-house Howard Cosell, was a leading proponent of getting rid of Knepper because he was a member of the born-again group.

> *Now he is on Gary Lavelle for the same reason. If Dickey has his way Lavelle (ERA 2.77) will be traded and in a few years Nevius or some other writer will chronicle another "foolish trade." How about trading Dickey?*[3]

In December 1984 Lavelle declined a trade to the Detroit Tigers, his right under Major League Baseball's rule that players who have accrued ten years of major league service time and spent the past five consecutive years with the same team can veto any trade scenario.

Prior to Lavelle's decision, Dickey wrote, "I hope the Giants can convince Gary Lavelle to accept the trade with Detroit. I like Lavelle and he has pitched well for the Giants. But he is the leader of the Born Again clique in the clubhouse that has to be broken up. As long as that clique remains, no matter what kind of players the Giants have, they'll be losers."[4]

Another *Chronicle* reader was fed up with Dickey's attack on the God Squadders. L. Marini wrote, "What is Glenn Dickey's gripe against born-again Christians? Would he rather they be into drugs and corruption? It seems the better you try to live, the more persecution you have to take. They hung a man on the cross who didn't have any sins—I bet Glenn Dickey would have been one of the leaders of that group."[5]

That didn't stop Dickey, however. In January 1985 he wrote:

> *When I talked to [General Manager Tom] Haller this week, he insisted that the Giants are a better team than they showed last year, and he's right.*
>
> *"The players have to kick themselves in the butt and get*

going," he said. "They have to say to themselves, 'Hey, I'm tired of being ridiculed. I'm going to do something about it.'"

But to change that attitude, Haller needs to clear out more of the losing personalities on the club. Moving LeMaster would be a good start. Trading off the over-priced prima donnas on the bullpen, Greg Minton and Gary Lavelle, would be another. Break up that clique that is comfortable with losing.[6]

That was an odd thing to write about Lavelle, considering the southpaw posted a 5–4 record with a 2.76 ERA and twelve saves in 1984, a season where the Giants were 66–96 and finished last in their division.

Lavelle didn't feel that the born-again players formed a clique.

"I think everybody had who you hung out with, or if the wives were friends with certain people, you would have meals and stuff like that," he said. "And not just Christians, but non-Christians as well, quite a few of the players and their wives. We would go out to dinner, and it didn't matter what their beliefs were. They were just friends and teammates."[7]

In April 1980, Lavelle's teammate Vida Blue, who at other times questioned the aggressiveness of the born-again players, said, "Clark, Lavelle, Ivie, Hill . . . None of those guys are really trying to convert anybody, but they let it be known they are Christians. Hey, maybe we should all take a long look at what they're saying. Maybe some of the rest of us have somethin' to hear."[8]

When Frank Robinson was hired to manage the Giants in 1981, Dan Shaughnessy of the *Washington Evening Star* wrote, " . . . around the Bay Area, it's a known fact that the Giants have been over .500 only twice since 1971 and haven't finished above third since winning the National League West that season. Worse, they are plagued by a 'God Squad' faction that necessitates two buses, one for the born-agains and one for the rest of the team."[9]

The *Fort Worth Star-Telegram* debunked that claim a few weeks later:

Relief pitcher Gary Lavelle, Chapel leader for the Giants, denies reports of separate buses, one for Christians and one for other players, or friction between the players.

"If there were factions or trouble it wasn't known to the players," Lavelle said. "I think most of it [the rumors] reflects back to the attitude of the media in the Bay Area. A few of us spoke out about our faith and gave the glory to Jesus Christ. When things started going bad, a few writers began saying that, because of our faith, we had become passive."[10]

Bill Shirley of the *Los Angeles Times* wrote in 1984:

Lavelle became a Christian eight years ago. When the Giants are at home, he holds monthly Bible study sessions at his home for five or six of his teammates and their wives. He denied reports that he and his group caused divisiveness on the team with their passive behavior. "There has never been any of that," he said. "The press blew it out of proportion."[11]

But as late at 1989, Mark Kram of the *Philadelphia Daily News* was repeating the separate buses falsehood: "The San

Francisco Giants had separate buses during the stewardship of Manager Joe Altobelli in the late '70s: one for the evangelicals, one for the non-evangelicals."[12]

Regarding that claim, Lavelle told this author in July 2023, "There is no truth to that statement."[13]

Perhaps the buses rumor started from this sarcastic remark by manager Dave Bristol in 1980: "There will be two buses to the ballpark . . . one at 2 for those who need extra work and the empty bus at 5 o'clock."[14]

Some fans were glad to see the God Squadders depart. In a letter to the editor in the *Chronicle* sports page in February 1985, under the heading, "Trade LeMaster Too," Janice Hanway wrote, "Now that crybaby Clark and Born-Again Lavelle have left, if the Giants will trade LeMaster, I may come out and watch them."[15]

Her wish came true. When the Giants traded LeMaster to the Cleveland Indians in May 1985, it marked the end of the original God Squad in San Francisco. Clark and Lavelle had been traded to the St. Louis Cardinals and the Toronto Blue Jays, respectively, before the 1985 season. Whitfield played ball in Japan for three years after his 1980 season with the Giants, then returned to the States as a Los Angeles Dodger in 1984. Knepper was traded to the Houston Astros after the 1980 season. Ivie also became an Astro, traded to Houston in April 1981. Andrews retired from the Giants and baseball after the 1979 season. Madlock was traded to Pittsburgh during the 1979 campaign, as was Roberts. Hill was traded to Seattle during the 1980 season. Moffitt signed with the Houston Astros as a free agent for the 1982 season. Herndon was traded to the Detroit Tigers and Griffin to the Pittsburgh Pirates before the 1982 season.

John Hillyer of the *Examiner*, in a straight news story

reporting on LeMaster's departure, managed to get in this dig: "LeMaster was the Giants' senior member, having broken in on Sept. 2, 1975. He was the last vestige of their so-called 'God Squad,' comprising players who, in the view of some observers, allowed their religious beliefs to get in the way of hard-nosed baseball and a winning attitude."[16]

Dickey made sure to kick the God Squadders on their way out, writing in January 1985:

> *The Giants are breaking up that old gang, and that's good news for all of us. Assuming the Jack Clark and Gary Lavelle trades go through, the Giants seem to have improved themselves. Though I hate to see Clark go, the club should have improved infield defense, more speed, marginally better pitching and left-handed power off the bench.*
>
> *But the most important factor is that the mental attitude of the club should be changed for the better. Lavelle, the leader of the divisive Born Again group, will be gone. The whining shortstop, Johnnie LeMaster, almost certainly will be traded. The energy that has been wasted on clubhouse bitching will be re-directed to the field.*[17]

But after they were gone, Dickey was still unhappy, writing on April 5, 1985:

> *For a time, it seemed the Giants were making progress in re-making the team. Jack Clark was traded for four players who could help. Gary Lavelle was traded, which took away the leader of the Born Again faction that has been so divisive in the clubhouse. But once again the Giants have confused a beginning with completion. Because nothing has been done since the Clark and Lavelle trades, this team still has serious flaws.*[18]

After Lavelle was traded to Toronto, Bob Padecky wrote:

Lavelle left San Francisco with some negative feelings, particularly on a much-used reference to his being the team leader of the "God Squad." A devout Christian, Lavelle had been accused of judging people harshly or of not giving a full effort.

"It hurts me to think about that," Lavelle said. "I'm not here to judge anyone. I don't try to force Jesus down anyone's throat. I've never tried to force anything down anyone's throat. I don't condemn anyone for what they do on or off the field. From my point of view as a Christian ballplayer, I should give 100 percent every time I'm on the field. I know I have."[19]

Dickey's wish had been granted. But a new cadre of Christians was growing on the Giants.

Notes

[1] Glenn Dickey, "Late Success Will Hurt the Giants," *San Francisco Chronicle*, September 7, 1984, 75.

[2] Glenn Dickey, "The Problem Is They've Never Had a Plan," *San Francisco Chronicle*, September 21, 1984, 77.

[3] Lou Thomas, "Letters to the Editor," *San Francisco Chronicle*, September 29, 1984, 45.

[4] Glenn Dickey, "The Message to Other A's in Rickey Trade," *San Francisco Chronicle*, December 7, 1984, 100.

[5] L. Marini, "Letters to the Editor," *San Francisco Chronicle*, December 15, 1984, 46.

[6] Glenn Dickey, "Clark Trade Is Necessary for Giants," *San Francisco Chronicle*, January 25, 1985, 79.

[7] Gary Lavelle, interview with author, June 1, 2023.

[8] Mike Granberry, "The Season According to Jack Clark," *Los Angeles Times*, April 10, 1980, 35.

[9] Dan Shaugnessy, "Giants Make F. Robby a Born-Again Manager," *Washington Evening Star*, January 15, 1981, 23.

[10] Jim Reeves, "Dugout Religion," *Fort Worth Star Telegram*, February 8, 1981, 37.

[11] Bill Shirley, "There Isn't Any Turning the Other Cheek," *Los Angeles Times*, November 1, 1984, 63.

[12] Mark Kram, "Religion and Sports," *Philadelphia Daily News*, November 2, 1988, 88.

[13] Gary Lavelle, interview with author, July 5, 2023.

[14] Russ Worman, "National League Preview," *Binghamton* (New York) *Press and Sun Bulletin*, April 5, 1981, 21.

[15] Janice Hanway, "Letters to the Green," *San Francisco Chronicle*, February 9, 1985, 44.

[16] John Hillyer, "LeMaster Traded to Indians," *San Francisco Examiner*, May 7, 1985, 47.

[17] Glenn Dickey, "Giants Deals Good in More Way than One," *San Francisco Chronicle*, January 28, 1985, 43.

[18] Glenn Dickey, "If Commercials Counted in the Standings," *San Francisco Chronicle*, April 5, 1985, 71.

[19] Bob Padecky, "Lavelle Fits the Mold as 'Happy Ex-Giant,'" *Reno* (Nevada) *Gazette-Journal*, March 18, 1985, 4-B.

Chapter 18
God Squad II

The second version of the God Squad included five pitchers—Atlee Hammaker, a Giant from 1982 to 1990, Scott Garrelts (1982–1991), Dave Dravecky (1987–1989), Jeff Brantley (1988–1993), and Craig Lefferts (1987–1989). Outfielders Brett Butler (1988–1990), Kevin Bass (1990–92), and Candy Maldonado (1986–1989), catcher Gary Carter (1990), and utility men Dave Anderson (1990–91) and Greg Litton (1989–92) were also born-again Giants. And Houston traded Bob Knepper back to the Giants in 1989.

When Knepper returned, Art Spander of the *Examiner* wrote this retrospective on the first God Squad:

> *The Giants were inexperienced in those days. The Giants were not very good in those days. The fans booed. The media criticized. Bob and others found solace in religion, their support in troubled times.*
>
> *They were an easy mark. We labeled them "The God Squad," and wondered exactly what belief in a higher authority had to do with justifying a hanging curve. They responded with the idea that in the great scheme of things baseball wasn't all that important. Someplace, sometime during 1980, after he gave up a home run, Knepper was quoted as saying, "It was God's will."*
>
> *He denied the specific statement. He stood fast to the philosophy, which was this: You do your best, and if it's not good enough, well then, Christianity advises, there's*

nothing more you can do.[1]

Knepper told Spander, "Things I've said probably cost me a lot, distracted me. I look at things a lot differently now. I hold the same Christian beliefs, but I am more tolerant. When I criticized the media and the fans I was young and felt I let everyone down. I reacted out of survival. I thought fans booed me because they didn't like me personally. I've learned they were booing my performance, not me."[2]

In September 1989, the *Santa Rosa Press Democrat* reported that as many as fifteen Giants out of the twenty-four-man base roster attended chapel services.

"It can be a source of great unity on a team," said Knepper, "but if the other guys have a real struggle with it, then it can cause a division."[3]

A year earlier, misunderstanding had grown between the God Squadders and some teammates, fed, in part, by the press. Dravecky described it:

> *I and three other pitchers—Scott Garrelts, Jeff Brantley, and Atlee Hammaker—had been up front about being believers, and we did not hide our faith under a bushel. The beat writers, always looking for something to write about, coined a term for our quartet, the "God Squad." They might as well have pinned bull's-eyes on the back of our uniforms for all the good it did us. Anything and everything we said could be interpreted by our teammates as "holier than thou." If we commented that we didn't go to R-rated movies with tons of nudity and sex, then our teammates thought we were judging them. If we said that we preferred to have a Bible study in our hotel rooms after a road game, that was interpreted as being anti-social by our teammates.*

After a while, the "God Squad" term became a pejorative. It certainly made life difficult for us in the clubhouse as reporters constantly probed other ballplayers about their feelings regarding the "religious" pitchers on their team. Scott, Jeff, Atlee, and I read anonymous quotes from our teammates questioning whether we had what it took to be winners. Some felt that we were too "passive" or "weak" because we shrugged off defeat, thinking it must have been "God's will."

That was a bunch of baloney because I know I fought with everything I had when I was on the mound . . . If the media has a weakness, it's called writing from the "template." The template for Christian ballplayers is that we are too nice to be winners, that we lack intensity and determination at crunch time, and that when we lose, we shrug our shoulders and mumble, "Praise the Lord."[4]

Henry Schulman, the Giants' beat writer for the *Oakland Tribune* at the time, strongly supports Dravecky's view. He told this author:

In dealing with the second wave of God Squadders, I never got the sense that they felt wins and losses had anything to do with God, Satan, or anything else besides how they play. That was a bum rap. That said, I always felt among these players a surety that their faith in God was rewarded in kind by the health and strength to perform to their abilities. You often hear players in postgame interviews thank God for their physical abilities and health.

There was nothing passive about any of the athletes I covered on the field, and I don't think their teammates felt that way either. Dravecky, Garrelts, Carter, and Brantley were among the most competitive I covered.[5]

Dravecky received support from his manager, Roger Craig. After the southpaw spun a two-hit, complete-game shutout against the Cardinals in Game 2 of the 1987 National League Championship Series, he was led to a media room next to the locker room where Craig was answering questions. When the manager looked up and saw Dravecky, he said, "They say Christians don't have any guts. Well, this guy's a Christian and he's not afraid of anything."[6]

Dravecky demonstrated that courage in a remarkable chain of events that began in 1988. He had surgery to remove a cancerous tumor in his pitching arm in October of that year. The operation involved removing half of the deltoid muscle and freezing the humerus bone in an attempt to eliminate all the cancerous cells. In what many called a miraculous return to baseball, Dravecky pitched eight-innings in a 4–3 victory over the Cincinnati Reds on August 10, 1989, at Candlestick Park in front of 34,810 roaring fans.

Writing in 1999 for the *Chronicle*, where he was the Giants' beat writer from 1998 until his retirement in 2020, Schulman recalled that game played ten years earlier:

> *Dravecky did not exactly fit the San Francisco mold. His politics were right of Ronald Reagan's, and he was a born-again Christian. But . . . when Dravecky returned to the mound at Candlestick Park for the first time after battling cancer in his arm for more than a year, everyone—politics and religion not withstanding—felt a kinship with the man.*
>
> *On a beautiful afternoon, with not a wisp of wind in the air, the applause began as soon as Dravecky stepped out of the tunnel to begin his pregame warmups. The applause turned into an ovation, one of many he got that day as he not only pitched, but won, beating the Cincinnati Reds. There were lumps in tens of thousands of throats.*[7]

However, Dravecky's post-game press conference made Lowell Cohn uncomfortable. After writing that "it's been my experience that the born-again Christians on the Giants sincerely try to live up to their religious ideals, and that men like LeMaster, Butler, Atlee Hammaker, Dave Dravecky and the rest are the most reasonable and patient baseball players you'll ever meet," Cohn continued, describing his conflicting feelings:

> *I had to admit that it would be fair to write about Dravecky's faith ... But I didn't mention God in my story ... I decided that Dravecky's polite and well-meaning sermon was too personal, that it was strictly a private matter between him and the deity. Perhaps I also thought it would have turned off readers. On the other hand, I know it's my job to give a true sense of what happened in that interview room ... So, here I am caught on the horns of a dilemma. I thought sportswriting wasn't supposed to be so complicated.*[8]

Five days after his big win, while pitching in Montreal, Dravecky felt a tingling sensation in his arm in the fifth inning. Then, in the sixth inning, on his first pitch to Tim Raines, Dravecky's humerus bone shattered, the sound heard throughout the stadium as Dravecky collapsed on the mound.

San Francisco Chronicle sportswriter Bruce Jenkins was amazed at Dravecky's equanimity when the pitcher met with the Bay Area press the morning after his injury. Jenkins wrote:

> *He had the same calm, relaxed look on his face, the same*

glow in his eye, the same attitude that said, "My life is going just great." That's the Dravecky we've always known, and it's the one we've got today. If you are put off by the open preachings of Christian athletes, then maybe his story is not for you. But Dravecky's beliefs are at the heart of his strength. That became abundantly clear in the wake of an injury that sent shock waves through the baseball world.[9]

Jenkins also noted how Dravecky's born-again teammates rallied around him when the pitcher returned to his hotel room the night of his injury. Jenkins wrote, "Within minutes, his best friends on the team were there: Garrelts, Bob Knepper, Jeff Brantley and Greg Litton. The five of them, all of whom share a vigorous belief in Christianity, stayed in Dravecky's room from midnight until 5 a.m., talking things over."

Dravecky's faith and courage had an impact on his other Giants teammates. Although he had felt there was division between the Christians and non-Christians in 1988, he said that was not a problem on the 1989 team.

"I think there's a camaraderie on this club," he said near the close of the 1989 regular season. "I also think there's a genuine respect from the players on the team that might not choose to attend (chapel), and that's obviously important."[10]

Knepper agreed, stating, "In this case, the Christians are respected. I feel our Christians are very open about their faith, and yet they're not shoving it down people's throats. They accept and understand that a lot of people may never accept the Christian faith."[11]

In 1990, Gary Swan of the *Chronicle* wrote:

> *The Giants, for a number of reasons, have a larger Christian presence than most teams.*
>
> *Pat Ritchie, an Evangelical Covenant Church Minister who organizes the Giants' [Sunday chapel] services, said the attendance had been bolstered by former pitcher Dave Dravecky's faith through his fight with cancer and the acquisition of players in the off-season who were chapel leaders with their previous teams — Carter, Jose Alvarez, Dave Anderson, Kevin Bass and Knepper, since released.*
>
> *An hour before game time on a recent Sunday, 19 of the Giants' 25 players gathered to listen to a Christian message and say prayers with pitcher Steve Bedrosian for the recovery of his leukemia-stricken son, Cody. That night, after the team lost to the Pittsburgh Pirates, 8–5, a dozen players and their wives went to a Bible-study session at a teammate's home.*
>
> *"Alvarez and Knepper have such a thorough knowledge of the Bible that if I were a pastor, I'd have no qualms in hiring them for my staff," Ritchie said.*[12]

Dravecky's cancer returned and his left arm and shoulder had to be amputated in June 1991. On July 16, the Associated Press reported on the first time Dravecky spoke publicly after the operation:

> *Looking fit and rested, Dravecky said, "There's adjustments that I have to make, but there's nothing out there that I don't want to do." ... Although his future won't include baseball, Dravecky said he will swim, play golf and tennis, and engage in other sports he was unable to enjoy in the past because of his baseball contract. He also has a full schedule of speaking engagements ...*

Appearing with his wife, Janice, at the Christian Booksellers Association annual convention in Orlando [Florida], Dravecky credited his religious faith for helping him overcome his cancer problems, which began in 1988. He said he is feeling extremely well despite "phantom pain" in his missing left hand and fingers—not an unusual occurrence in amputees.[13]

Dravecky did have one regret about his time in the big leagues:

Playing for the Padres and the Giants during the time I did when the "God Squad" was a big deal, the reality is that my teammates were extremely respectful of where we were at on our journey. I'm very grateful for the respect that my teammates showed us as we were attempting to lead out our lives as Christians, which we didn't do perfectly.

If I were to do anything different, I would have probably spent more time in bars. Often I got invited by guys who simply wanted to go out, grab a beer, get something to eat—usually that was at the bar—and just hang out. I said, "No, cant' go there." And that's exactly where Jesus went and that's exactly where I should have been because I didn't have an issue with whether or not I was going to drink too much. I knew when to say no. And quite frankly, here's a guy who wants to spend time with me and I'm saying I can't go into the bar. "Well, here we go the Holy Roller."

If there's any regret it would have been engaging more with everybody in the clubhouse. That was just a period of time in my life where I was young and dumb. I didn't get it.[14]

Garrelts, who had given his life to Jesus in 1984, said his faith grew when the Padres traded Dravecky to the Giants in 1987 and Butler arrived from Cleveland the following year. Those three plus Hammaker began to meet weekly to study the Bible and pray for each other. Knepper joined the group when he arrived in 1989.

Butler was a fiery ballplayer, and he told this author about an on-field incident that tested his character.

In 1987, when I was with the Indians, we were playing the Royals in Kansas City, and things really got out of hand. The previous night, the Royals' Willie Wilson was ejected from the game for tackling our pitcher Ken Schromm after a pitch came close to Wilson's head. I should have expected trouble as I stepped to the plate, the first batter of the game that evening. I dug in to face hard-throwing Danny Jackson, and his first pitch sailed behind my head. I thought, okay, the guy threw at me one time. I'll let it go. No big deal.

But then came the second pitch—right behind my head again! Well, the human side of me came out. I charged the mound. I threw some punches. Both Danny and I were ejected from the game.[15]

Butler jammed his thumb during the fight, causing him to miss four games. He was suspended for another three.

"That gave me plenty of time to think about what I had done," said Butler. "I asked myself, as a Christian, how do I handle that situation? I realized that the Lord tells us to turn the other cheek, so I repented, 'Lord, forgive me for this.' Then, out of that attitude, I did the things that needed to be done."[16]

Butler approached Jackson and apologized, as did Jackson, and they became friends.

"I think we can learn a lot from our mistakes," Butler reflected. "If somebody threw at me again, I'm not saying I would just get up and go to first base. Frankly, I don't know what I'd do. But I feel I would be able to handle it in a better manner than I did."[17]

When Butler signed with the Dodgers in 1991, his passionate style of play rubbed off on his new teammates. In August 1991, Bruce Jenkins of the *Chronicle* wrote:

> *So much has revolved around Butler. Everybody but the Giants appreciated what he can do, and if you had to name a National League MVP today, he would be right up there with Terry Pendleton, Barry Bonds, Bobby Bonilla, Howard Johnson and Will Clark. Butler has brought a strong Christian influence to the clubhouse and when born-again Darryl Strawberry went into the tank, Butler told him it was OK to get mad.*
>
> *"I told him to get his fire back," said Butler. "You can be a Christian and still be a hard-nosed player. God doesn't say you can't get mad or frustrated. Jesus flipped tables in the temple."*
>
> *Strawberry took to the advice, hitting six home runs in the next couple of weeks. Interestingly, if the Dodgers were to go all the way, they would be the first team with an overriding Christian influence (Butler, Strawberry, Hershiser, Gary Carter [who, like Butler, was granted free agency by the Giants after the 1990 season and signed by the Dodgers for the 1991 season]) to do so. Only in baseball could the merits of such a development be questioned.*[18]

The Dodgers narrowly missed the postseason that year, finishing one game behind the Atlanta Braves.

Notes

[1] Art Spander, "Knepper Will Be Judged on Performance," *San Francisco Examiner*, August 6, 1989, 37, 44.

[2] Art Spander, "Knepper Will Be Judged on Performance," *San Francisco Examiner*, August 6, 1989, 37.

[3] Larry Stone, "Ten Years Later, God Squad Makes Comeback," *Santa Rosa Press Democrat*, September 24, 1989, C-3.

[4] Dave Dravecky and Mike Yorkey, *Called Up: Stories of Life and Faith from the Great Game of Baseball* (Grand Rapids, MI: Zondervan, 2004), 162–63, 174.

[5] Henry Schulman, interview with author, June 5, 2023.

[6] Dave Dravecky and Mike Yorkey, *Called Up: Stories of Life and Faith from the Great Game of Baseball* (Grand Rapids, MI: Zondervan, 2004), 175.

[7] Henry Schulman, "Dravecky Footage Shows Horror, Misses Heart," *San Francisco Chronicle*, June 1, 1999, 47.

[8] Lowell Cohn, "A Question of Religion," *San Francisco Chronicle*, August 15, 1989, 46.

[9] Bruce Jenkins, "Spirit Still Infuses Dravecky," *San Francisco Chronicle*, August 17, 1989, D-1.

[10] Larry Stone, "Ten Years Later, God Squad Makes Comeback," *Santa Rosa Press Democrat*, September 24, 1989, C-3.

[11] Larry Stone, "Ten Years Later, God Squad Makes Comeback," *Santa Rosa Press Democrat*, September 24, 1989, C-3.

[12] Gary Swan, "God and Baseball," *San Francisco Chronicle*, August 14, 1990, D-3.

[13] Associated Press, "Dravecky Starts His New Life," *San Francisco Chronicle*, July 16, 1991, 25.

[14] Jacob Unruh, "Collected Wisdom: Former Major League Baseball Player Dave Dravecky," *The Oklahoman*, March 1, 2015, 2.

[15] Brett Butler with Matt Sieger, "A Rock to Lean On," *Voice*, July 1989, 32.

[16] Brett Butler with Matt Sieger, "A Rock to Lean On," *Voice*, July 1989, 32.

[17] Brett Butler with Matt Sieger, "A Rock to Lean On," *Voice*, July 1989, 32.

[18] Bruce Jenkins, "An Update on Contenders in NL West," *San Francisco Chronicle*, August 5, 1991, 20.

Chapter 19
Satan and Brett Butler

In 1983, Glenn Dickey wrote, "Having heard Born Again athletes praise the Lord for their home runs, touchdown passes, ad nauseum, I'm waiting for the day one of them fumbles and says, 'The Devil made me do it.'"[1]

His wish was granted—sort of—seven years later.

Butler found himself in hot water with the press in 1990. On Monday, May 7, the *Oakland Tribune* ran a front-page (of the paper, not just the sports page) headline which read, "Giants' Losing Ways. The Devil Made Them Do It." Henry Schulman interviewed Butler for the article. Schulman wrote:

> Manager Roger Craig says the Giants are being tested this year, and center fielder Brett Butler knows by whom. It's Satan, Butler said.
>
> "I have no doubt in my mind. I just think when there is an abundance of believers brought together, at times there's going to be a war coming out of it," Butler said . . .
>
> By believers, Butler means "born-again" Christians like himself and several others on the Giants, including catcher Gary Carter, infielder Greg Litton and pitchers Bob Knepper, Atlee Hammaker and Scott Garrelts.
>
> "I think," Butler said, "Satan sometimes attacks those who are strong in the Lord."
>
> Butler said he did not mean the team's bad play on the field was a result of intervention from below. Comments

like that were attributed in the late '70s and early '80s to Giants on the so-called "God Squad," leading to criticism they were not as competitive as they should be because they believed in predestination.[2]

The headline was off base, as the article specifically stated that Butler did not believe Satan was responsible for the Giants' slow start to the season. Also, checking on Schulman's assertion, this author could not find any articles in which any of the original God Squad Giants attributed subpar play to the devil.

That Monday night, before the game in Montreal, Butler asked to meet with the six writers who covered the Giants to address the *Tribune* article.

The next day, Larry Stone wrote in the *San Francisco Examiner*:

More than a decade after the Giants' so-called "God Squad" became a cause celebre in the Bay Area, religion and baseball have once again been linked in their clubhouse. In a published report Monday, Brett Butler said he felt the team was being tested by Satan because of the large number of born-again Christians on the team. In a press conference in manager Roger Craig's office before the Giants' Monday night game in Montreal, Butler stressed he wasn't blaming the Giants' poor performance on the devil.

"I think something was taken out of context of what I was trying to say," Butler said. "I said, 'I guess the Lord has brought warriors together, a lot of Christians on this club, to fight a battle. Because I believe Satan is really doing a toll on us.'

"In saying that, I meant as a whole, not just the ball-

club. I believe Satan fires on everyone in the world, every day. But that is not the reason for our [the Giants] fall. The reason for our fall is because we are injury-plagued, because our pitchers aren't doing the job, and our hitters aren't doing the job. It has nothing to do with Satan making a fall on this ballclub."³

Schulman wrote, "Other born-again Christians on the club are hesitant to speak out like Butler, but not because they disagree with him. Garrelts said he was afraid people would misunderstand them, wrongly assuming that players believe that what happens on the field is God's will or the work of Satan. 'But I know as a Christian you are always under attack from Satan,' Garrelts said."⁴

Carter came to Butler's defense, saying, "I feel very strongly I was led to this team because of the strong believers here. I can understand Bugsy's [Butler's] reasoning, very much so. In our daily lives, we're tested all the time. I justify what Bugsy feels. I know his belief is strong."⁵

Knepper, then on his second Giants God Squad, said he had learned some lessons from his first go-round:

> I was here through the wars in the late '70s, when everything hit the fan. If you're making a story that can cause a lot of controversy, nothing good can come out of anything I can say. I just don't think the newspaper is the place to discuss spiritual matters, especially one as sensitive as strong Christian beliefs in an area as schizo about Christian beliefs as the Bay Area. I know how easy it is for things that make sense to Christians to get blown out of the water.

He added, "I'm sure there'll be a lot of interesting columns out there."⁶

Knepper was right. Rob Morse wrote in the *Examiner*:

You bet, Brett. With communism on the way out, Satan has a lot of time on his hands so he's running his own little rotisserie league—and it's the Giants who are on the rotisserie, scorched by the fires of hell and unhittable inside fastballs. You can imagine Satan saying, "The only way the Giants will get to the World Series this year is by paying admission, but Brett Butler is strong in the Lord, so I'll just move Wade Boggs and Pete Rose to the back burner."

In baseball, trouble usually comes down to fundamentals. This time it's come down to fundamentalists—ones who can't hit the theological cut-off man. Ask yourself, with George Steinbrenner in baseball, why would Satan pay any attention to Brett Butler?[7]

Also in the *Examiner*, John C. Dvorak wrote:

Satan is the issue around the Giants' locker room. If you haven't been following the latest glorious episode in a long history of self-righteous Bible thumping amongst people who have played for the Giants, you should. Centerfielder Brett Butler believes many of the Giants' woes are due to Satan. He admits that the pitching and hitting could be better, but is convinced, for example, that the nasty old earthquake during the World Series was clearly the work of Satan.

. . . When I read all this craziness, imagining the great battle of good vs. evil, I begin to wonder why the Giants have always had guys like Butler on the team. The God Squad. What's with these guys—do they believe that Satan is their 10th man?[8]

Bud Geracie of the *San Jose Mercury News*, commenting

on Schulman's article, wrote:

> *I know Brett Butler well enough to know he wasn't joking. I don't know him well enough to know what he meant. Can we really blame the devil for what's happening to the Giants? No, Butler said. But his words kept saying yes, every time I read them Monday morning . . . My guess is that Butler meant what he said, before he started making qualifications and confusion.*[9]

Geracie added, "I don't mean to make light of Butler's beliefs, whatever they may be. But you don't need to look far to see what's wrong with the Giants. Their pitching is lousy, and that has come as no surprise to anybody outside the Giants family."[10]

Bob Padecky of the *Santa Rosa* (California) *Press Democrat* chimed in:

> *Earlier this week, center fielder Brett Butler said he thought the Giants were under attack from Satan. I don't know if he's right or if he's wrong. But I do know he should have kept his opinion to himself.*
>
> *. . . most Christians I have met in sports have learned to keep their Christianity to themselves. Not that they are embarrassed by it. Far from it. They don't mind talking about it—but they are perfectly comfortable NOT talking about it. They are respectful of others and their right to worship, knowing others may not believe the same way and that it may be insulting to have a belief other than their own forced down their throat.*[11]

Lowell Cohn was not about to let this golden opportunity

slip by. In his column, "Giants Have an Enemy in Low Places," he wrote:

> I suppose you have a theory about what's wrong with the Giants. It's probably some mundane analysis—like the Giants' pitching stinks and the team can't score runs when it counts. Well, you're all wet. It's just possible that the devil is the Giants' problem.. . . . it just so happens that I came across a memo the devil penned to himself . . . In flaming red ink, Satan had written, "Things to do: Take laundry to dry cleaners. Lay off the pepperoni pizza . . . But the main thing is those Giants. Cannot tolerate success by such a bunch of do-gooders. Especially important to irritate the born-agains—Brett Butler, Atlee Hammaker, Scott Garrelts, Gary Carter, Bob Knepper and Greg Litton."[12]

Glenn Dickey also got into the act. When Butler appeared headed to a new club in free agency after the 1990 season, Dickey wrote, "Perhaps Butler will eventually get more money elsewhere than he could have got with the Giants, but he's leaving a winning club where he seemed to be happy, even if he couldn't shake Satan."[13]

Schulman discussed with this author how the column came about and Butler's reaction to it:

> We were sitting in the dugout in Montreal at a time when the Giants got hit by a lot of injuries at once, Butler came by during batting practice and said words to the effect of, "Satan sure likes to attack groups that have a lot of crusaders," meaning crusaders for Christ. I got him alone later and asked him what he meant and he explained it, so I wrote it.
>
> The real problem was the headline: "Giants' Losing

Ways: The Devil Made Them Do It." That's not what he said. Butler specifically said he did not think they were losing because of some black force. He got ridiculed in national media and was very angry with me for the whole thing, particularly the headline, which of course I did not write. It blew over after a while. I think there were a lot of eyerolls in the clubhouse to what he said.[14]

Schulman also shared an amusing anecdote about Butler:

At Candlestick, once the game was over the media had to run to the lone stadium elevator all the way down the right-field line to get down to the clubhouse. If we missed the first elevator, it would take a long time for it to return and take you down again, which meant you might miss the manager's postgame news conference.

That happened to me one night, and when I got to the elevator I cursed up a blue streak, unaware that several player wives were behind me waiting for the same elevator.

Butler pulled me aside the next day—this was after we made peace—and said, "Henry, Eveline [Butler's wife] told me what happened at the elevator. Listen, we're okay with the 'm-fs' and the other words you used, but please don't say 'g-d.' " That's how he said it, in that shorthand.[15]

Knepper was correct. Often Christians and non-Christians are speaking different languages—literally and figuratively. That was a major reason for the tension between the press and the born-again Giants on God Squads I and II.

Since that time, Christian athletes are more accepted by the press, the public, and their teammates. Some ballclubs, like the St Louis Cardinals, hold a Christian Day each season, where the Christian Cards speak about their faith after the game. The Giants hold an annual Fellowship Day which they co-sponsor with the Salvation Army. Fans are treated to a post-game concert in the ballpark and a question-and-answer session with players and coaches on how their faith has shaped their game.

As Chris Smith wrote in *The New York Times* in 1997:

> *The evangelical presence in sports has been gathering momentum since the late 70's, when teams like the Los Angeles Dodgers were known for a strong moralistic bent. But in those days, born-again athletes were often ridiculed as wimps, and the noisiest religious demonstration at sporting events was usually a guy in a rainbow wig flashing a John 3:16 sign for TV cameras. Now, thanks largely to decades of aggressive spadework at the high-school and college levels by groups like the Fellowship of Christian Athletes, vocal Christian players are nearing a majority in professional sports, particularly in golf, football and baseball.*[16]

Athletes have also become more sensitive, in general, in how they express their faith. That, in turn, gives sportswriters less to pounce on. As Gary Swan of the *Chronicle* wrote in 1990, "It does seem that religious fervor on major league clubs has met with general acceptance ... It is rare to hear a complaint voiced years ago by managers that Christian ballplayers found it too easy to accept losing or too hard to do some of baseball's dirty work."[17]

Notes

[1] Glenn Dickey, "49ers Can Catch Cowboys on Rebound," *San Francisco Chronicle*, December 6, 1983, 47.

[2] Henry Schulman, "Giants' Losing Ways: The Devil Made Them Do It," *Oakland Tribune*, May 7, 1990, A-1, A-12.

[3] Larry Stone, "Butler: I Was Misinterpreted," *San Francisco Examiner*, May 8, 1990, 25.

[4] Henry Schulman, "Giants' Losing Ways: The Devil Made Them Do It," *Oakland Tribune*, May 7, 1990, A-12.

[5] Larry Stone, "Butler: I Was Misinterpreted," *San Francisco Examiner*, May 8, 1990, 31.

[6] Ray Ratto, "Butler Denies Statements on Satan," *San Francisco Chronicle*, May 8, 1990, D-5.

[7] Rob Morse, "Isn't that Conveeenient [sic]?" *San Francisco Examiner*, May 8, 1990, A-3.

[8] John C. Dvorak, "Satan Now At Bat for the Giants," *San Francisco Examiner*, May 14, 1990, 19.

[9] Bud Geracie, "What the Devil is Wrong with Giants?" *San Jose Mercury News*, published in *Sacramento Bee*, May 9, 1990, F-2.

[10] Bud Geracie, "What the Devil is Wrong with Giants?" *San Jose Mercury News*, published in *Sacramento Bee*, May 9, 1990, F-2.

[11] Bob Padecky, "A Touchy Subject Rears Its Horns," *Santa Rosa Press Democrat*, May 11, 1990, 21.

[12] Lowell Cohn, "Giants Have an Enemy in Low Places," *San Francisco Chronicle*, May 8, 1990, D-1.

[13] Glenn Dickey, "Getting McGee was Great Move by Rosen," *San Francisco Examiner*, December 5, 1990, D-3.

[14] Henry Schulman, interview with author, June 5, 2023.

[15] Henry Schulman, interview with author, June 5, 2023.

[16] Chris Smith, "God is an .800 Hitter," *The New York Times Magazine*, July 27, 1997, Section 6, 26.

[17] Gary Swan, "God and Baseball," *San Francisco Chronicle*, August 14, 1990, D-3.

Chapter 20
God Squad III?

Brett Butler believes that the Giants organization intentionally got rid of the born-again players on God Squads I and II.
As a Dodger, he told the Associated Press in 1991:

> *I think the fact that Christians come out and stand up for their belief now is more so than it was in the early 1950s and 1960s. And in turn, I think it has hurt some believers because a particular organization does not believe in that. The San Francisco Giants years ago had the "God Squad" and there were some negative situations involved there. That also happened in the last three or four years over there, and the number of believers on the club in San Francisco, in turn, have all been cut away or diminished or traded or released or whatever.*[1]

Gary Lavelle, after being traded to the Toronto Blue Jays, was quoted on the subject in an article by the *Chronicle's* Bruce Jenkins in May 1985:

> *Ex-Giant Gary Lavelle, bothered by a sore elbow recently, relieved Toronto starter Dave Stieb in the seventh inning and struck out two batters. Earlier, he had joked about the criticism of "born-again" players in the Giants clubhouse. "They got rid of Jack (Clark) and me, but I don't see a whole lot of difference," he said. "I'm sure Johnnie (LeMaster) is*

next." About an hour later, it was announced that LeMaster had been traded to Cleveland.[2]

Regarding the Giants' trade of Knepper to Houston, Vida Blue said, "I felt bad for him because they made such a fuss about him being a born-again Christian and all that stuff and claimed he lost his competitive edge. I think the Christian thing allowed people to be critical of him in the press. When he was on the field, I like to think he was giving 100 percent, but some people didn't think so, so he was traded."[3]

Rob Andrews, released by the Giants in 1979, told the *San Francisco Examiner*:

> *I have no ill feelings toward (Giants' owner) Bob Lurie or (general manager) Spec Richardson. Business is strictly business. Management isn't going to care if they uproot your family by trading you the day before the season starts. They're not going to care if you're a "good guy" or someone who isn't well-liked by the teammates. But I think that my involvement with the Christian Giants and the criticism the front office got for that, as well as the team's overall performance, was a factor in their releasing me.*[4]

Did Giants management make a deliberate effort to discard the born-again Christian ballplayers? Was the front office swayed by Dickey's constant urging to "break up that clique"? That's a difficult accusation to prove. One would hope that general managers make trades or release players based on ability and financial considerations. As was mentioned, the Giants acquired several players in the late 1980s who were chapel leaders on their previous teams.

The Giants have also had their share of born-again

believers since those days, including Felipe Alou, who managed the team from 2003 to 2006. But the local press has never dubbed another bunch the God Squad.

Alou was in the middle of controversy in 2005 when KNBR radio sports talk host Larry Krueger made reference to the Giants' "brain-dead Caribbean hitters hacking at slop nightly." Alou, who was raised in the Dominican Republic and was inducted into the Caribbean Baseball Hall of Fame in 2016, was none too pleased. When asked on ESPN's "Outside the Lines" program if he would forgive Krueger, Alou called Krueger "this messenger of Satan, as I call this guy now ... And I believe there is no forgiveness for Satan." But Alou told ESPN he did not want Krueger fired for his comments about Caribbean ballplayers.[5]

The next morning, KNBR made fun of Alou's statement, parodying it with Satan references from "South Park" and "Saturday Night Live." That evening, KNBR management fired Krueger, program director Bob Agnew, and Tony Rhein, producer of KNBR's morning show.[6]

After the firings, Alou said, "I think it is very unfortunate that a man, or a number of men, had to lose their jobs over a thing like this. It was not my objective. My objective has always been for people to understand this is a social issue, and to make people aware that this is not to be tolerated, to degrade a race of people or people from a region."[7]

The original God Squad caused a stir for a few reasons. The public was not accustomed to athletes openly declaring their faith. As Brett Butler said, Christianity had been much more private in previous decades. Bobby Richardson, the former president of Baseball Chapel who played in the 1950s and 1960s for the New York Yankees, said, "It was uncommon in those early days for players to take a stand."[8]

Bay Area residents, many of whom are liberal in politics and accepting of sexual orientation, may have felt antagonistic toward the God Squadders, conflating their values with those of other Christian groups they felt were judgmental. Finally, the God Squadders encountered local columnists, two in particular in Cohn and Dickey, who were excellent wordsmiths and loved to write controversial pieces. The God Squad was fodder for their often biting sarcasm.

It is unlikely that Bay Area sportswriters, ballplayers, and readers will ever again experience baseball seasons as controversial and fascinating as those of the original God Squad.

Notes

[1] Jim Donaghy, "Religious Players Not on Crusade," *Orange County* (California) *Register*, July 28, 1991, 51.

[2] Bruce Jenkins, "Wind-Aided Rout—A's Blown Away by the Jays, 10-1," *San Francisco Chronicle*, May 8, 1985, 63.

[3] John Lindblom, "A Heck of a Good Season for Knepper in Houston," *Sunday Mercury News*, September 13, 1981, 53.

[4] John Kawamoto, "Ex-Giant Rob Andrews Reborn as Youth Pastor," *San Francisco Examiner*, April 22, 1981, 75.

[5] Steve Kroner, "Firings a Hot Topic," *San Francisco Chronicle*, August 11, 2005, 40.

[6] Steve Kroner, "KNBR Makes the Call: Krueger is Fired," *San Francisco Chronicle*, August 10, 2005, 32, 34.

[7] Steve Kroner, "Firings a Hot Topic," *San Francisco Chronicle*, August 11, 2005, 40.

[8] Gary Swan, "Baseball Chapel Offers Alternatives to Players," *San Francisco Chronicle*, August 14, 1990, D-3.

Afterword

In 1889, Oscar Wilde wrote, "Life imitates Art far more than Art imitates Life."[1]

But that was before computer simulation baseball games.

After completing this book, I was inspired to play one game between the 1978 Giants and the 1978 Dodgers on my favorite computer baseball game, Oldtime Baseball by Stormfront Studios, published in 1995.

The lineups were those used most frequently by the two teams that year. The starting pitchers were Burt Hooton, who won nineteen games for the Dodgers and posted a 2.71 ERA in 1978, and Bob Knepper for the Giants. The Giants were the home team and, just for fun, I played the game at Seals Stadium, the minor league park in San Francisco where the Giants played their first two seasons in 1958 and 1959.

I managed the Giants while the computer managed the Dodgers.

Knepper shut down the Dodgers for seven innings and took a 2–0 lead into the eighth. One of the Giants' runs was supplied by a solo homer from Terry Whitfield. The Dodgers reached Knepper for two runs in the eighth, so I brought in righthander Randy Moffitt, who yielded a hit, putting two runners on base with two outs and the score knotted at 2–2. With left-handed hitting Rick Monday coming to the plate, I brought in southpaw Gary Lavelle, who induced a flyout to end the threat.

In the bottom of the eighth, the Giants got two runners

aboard with two outs. Lavelle's spot was due up in the lineup, so I pinch hit Mike Ivie for him.

If you read this book, you can guess what Ivie did.

That's right! He hit a three-run homer to give the Giants a 5–2 lead. John Curtis came on in relief of Lavelle for a 1-2-3 ninth inning to secure the victory for San Francisco.

Lavelle got the win in relief. Knepper recorded ten strike-outs.

Whatever you may think of the God Squadders, I think we can all agree on one thing—they could play some ball.

Notes

[1] Oscar Wilde, *The Decay of Lying* (Richmond, Surrey, United Kingdom: Alma Books, 1891), 101.

Acknowledgments

In treating such a sensitive subject, I am grateful to the ballplayers, Gary Lavelle and Bob Knepper, and journalists, Lowell Cohn and Henry Schulman, for allowing me to interview them for this book. The "members" of the two versions of the God Squad (which formed in the late 1970s and again in the late 1980s) at times had an adversarial relationship with the press, and both Cohn and Schulman were, on occasion, in the thick of it.

It would have been easy for both of them to sidestep my request for their input, given the controversial topic and the many years that have passed. Even if they agreed to chat with me, I did not know what to expect. What were there true feelings about the born-again Christians on the Giants? Did they harbor hostility toward them? Or perhaps toward me, since I informed both of them that I too am a born-again believer in Jesus?

What I discovered, after they both graciously agreed to answer my questions, was that neither Cohn nor Schulman have any animosity toward the players or me or Christians in general. Both were just plying their trade. Cohn, as a columnist, had more leeway to be creative, and his main tool was satire. But readers who have perused any portion of the over 8,000 columns he penned in his career know that anybody and everybody were targets. When Cohn wrote about the born-again Giants—and he seldom did—he treated them with equal-opportunity sarcasm and wit.

Similarly, Schulman, whose game story coverage of the

Giants in the *San Francisco Chronicle* was outstanding, rarely waded into the born-again waters. In fact, his article that generated so much heat concerning Brett Butler and Satan was a straight sports interview, which the *Oakland Tribune* elected to run on the front page. Schulman just reported what Butler said, and he did so accurately.

I want to thank them for their openness and honesty with me.

On the other side of the coin, Lavelle and Knepper had good reason to not want to lend their voices to this book. Both had been burned by Bay Area sportswriters back in the late seventies and early eighties. Knepper in particular had been badly misrepresented, especially over the fictional "God's will" quote. Why would they trust another journalist—me—to get the facts right this time around?

But both Knepper and Lavelle put their feet back into the water and gave thoughtful answers to my initial and follow-up questions. They too, were very open and honest.

I hope that this book in some way helps to explain to each "side" of the controversy where the other side was coming from. There are, indeed, some bad apples, in both professional baseball and professional journalism, but I think these four—Lavelle, Knepper, Cohn, and Schulman—were all just trying to do their jobs. And they did them well.

I would also like to thank Pastor Lloyd Mashore for allowing me to interview him. From our chat, I can tell he has the true heart of a pastor, getting personally involved with the God Squadders when they needed him.

Speaking of pastors, I want to thank Terry Reilley, former pastor of Creekside Church in Martinez, California, for his encouragement and support as I wrote this book. I fed him my chapters as I went along, and he was an eager and appreciative audience. And a big thank you to Pastor Duane Adamson, a great friend who believed in me and gave me the book, *The Business of Being a Writer*, over forty years ago. I have written many magazine articles since then, but I have always wanted to apply the lessons of that volume to writing a book. And now this is my first.

My first work in print was at age fourteen when my junior high school English teacher, Joanne Hornick, published a book called *Creative Bulletin Boards* and asked me to write a few humorous sentences for one of her bulletin board concepts. Mrs. Hornick, who was my teacher in the seventh and eighth grades, was my favorite and inspired me to write.

A thank you also to the San Francisco Giants, who supplied me with those nice photographs of the God Squadders.

I appreciate my three former newspaper colleagues, Richard Bammer, Matt O'Donnell, and Thomas Gase, for taking the time to read the book and write their endorsements. The latter two are sports reporters, and I learned a lot from them.

Thank you to David Bartke, for his copyediting and friendship.

I also want to acknowledge my dad, who instilled in me my love for baseball, which was central to our relationship. He took me to see the New York Mets at the Polo Grounds in 1962, their inaugural season, and I have been a Mets fan ever since. We went to see the San Francisco Giants play the Mets at the Polo Grounds on "Willie Mays Night," May 3, 1963, with 49,4321 in attendance. I asked my dad, who had been a New York Giants fan from the days of Mel Ott, Bill Terry, and Carl Hubbell, who he would be rooting for. He said, "The Mets and Willie Mays."

About the Author

Matt Sieger has a B.A. from Cornell University and a master's degree in magazine journalism from Syracuse University's Newhouse School of Public Communications. He was a sports reporter for the *Cortland* (New York) *Standard*, *The* (Vacaville, California) *Reporter*, and the *Martinez* (California) *News-Gazette*. He is a Jewish believer in Jesus and, coincidentally, was born again the same summer this book highlights—1978.

ABOOKS

ALIVE Book Publishing and ALIVE Publishing Group
are imprints of Advanced Publishing LLC,
3200 A Danville Blvd., Suite 204, Alamo, California 94507

Telephone: 925.837.7303
alivebookpublishing.com